The Ten Commitments of Love

To: CAPPY, 9/20/08

:-) M. Hack

The Ten Commitments of Love

A Journal for Life on Planet Earth

Michele Mack

COVENANT OF LIGHT PUBLISHING

Covenant of Light Publishing
119 Mertz Road,
Mertztown, PA 19539 USA

First printing 1999

10   9   8   7   6   5   4   3   2   1

Manufactured in the United States of America
Printed on Acid-free Recycled Paper

Cover and Interior Design by Lightbourne

Library of Congress Catalog Card Number: 98-093707
ISBN: 0-9667747-0-1

The following publishers have generously given permission to use
extended quotations from copyrighted works:

The Complete Ascension Manual, by Joshua David Stone, Ph.D.
Copyright 1994, by Joshua David Stone. Reprinted by
permission of Light Technology Publishing.

Hidden Mysteries, by Joshua David Stone, Ph.D.
Copyright 1995, by Joshua David Stone. Reprinted by
permission of Light Technology Publishing.

Acknowledgments

*F*irst and last, I wish to acknowledge God. The source of all that is and of life itself. It does not matter what name you call the source. The source will always be the creator of all that exists.

In this space, I humbly wish to thank all my guides, angels, Hierarchy councils and beings of light, whose love, guidance and wisdom have helped me in every aspect of my life. I am honored to have worked with them and channel these inspirational words. I know these messages will touch the lives of all human beings who are open to receive this knowledge. My guides have helped me make my contribution to planet Earth.

I wish to send loving thanks to my parents, Leonard and Louise Mack. They have constantly supported the many endeavors I embarked on throughout my life. They have given me life, then set me free to make of it as I wish. Their unending array of love has always given me the encouragement to follow my dreams and be who I am. Thank you, Mom and Dad, for allowing me the freedom to live those dreams.

I thank my grandparents in spirit, Alphonse and Florence Caruso and Philip and Anne Mack. They have supported and encouraged me via the spirit world. I will never forget their words of wisdom: "Michele, don't ever give up. Just keep on trying and don't let anyone tell you that you can't succeed!" Those wonderful words of wisdom have helped me over the highest obstacles and guided me along the roughest roads. They have watched me grow from birth and lovingly laid the foundation for the journey of my life. I thank them dearly and know that they are only a telepathic call away.

I also thank my sister and brother, Lisa and Philip Mack. We have many childhood memories of times filled with fun as well as the frivolous fighting that kids do. Now, as adults, we've learned to share the toys and not fight over who owns them.

I would like to acknowledge other members of my family who made the holidays, picnics and gatherings a wonderful meeting place for all who attended. I thank Michael and Judy Caruso, Janine and John Lang, and Matthew Caruso. I have many fond memories of sitting at that dining room table with them and talking and laughing over the stories of our lives.

Next, I wish to acknowledge the Mack family. My aunts, Phyllis, Irene and Loretta. My cousins, Kathy, Joe, Drew, Katie, Eric, Ronnie and Philip. There are many fond memories of holidays spent at Grandma's house, especially Thanksgiving. These memories remain in my heart, and every now and then are recalled to my conscious mind. Also, I lovingly dedicate this book to the memory of my cousin, Richard Kieltyka. We all miss and love him. Richard will be remembered for his heart of gold—for he has touched many lives.

I want to thank the people at St. John's metaphysical church of faith in Allentown, Pa. I am grateful for the gifts I have received from all these wonderful people to numerous to mention. This is where my spiritual teachings and awakening began. Three of the main people responsible for these teachings include: Rev. Lloyd Moll, Rev. Isabelle Moll and Rev. Anna Kresley. This church was founded to embrace the truths of all religions in order to expand awareness throughout the world, revering all life for the benefit of all mankind. Who ever enters the door, is welcome. I believe the love that emanates from this little church is the beacon of light for all the surrounding areas.

I wish to acknowledge my spiritual circle of friends who include Sue Allen, Jolan Friend, Rev. Dee Stevens, Rev. Karen Kohler, Kathy DeVito, Bonnie Drabick and Dave Kolb. My friends have been there for me and filled my life with love, support and understanding. I am blessed to work with them to combine our energies on behalf of world peace and a new vision for planet Earth.

I would especially like to thank one of my spiritual friends, Bonnie Drabick. Bonnie has been a constant source of love, support and inspiration. Bonnie has helped within this physical plane to keep me going and has taught me not to give up. Her endless generosity and limitless giving are deeply appreciated.

I wish to thank all those who helped prepare this book for publication: Paula Martin, Shannon Bodie, Gaelyn Larrick and Margaret Pinyan.

Finally, a very special thanks to all the bookstores and bookclubs that carry this book. Your contribution and impact to the awakening of the people on planet Earth is monumental. You are the final messengers to cast this book across land and sea for all those who are ready and waiting with open hearts.

Contents

Acknowledgments . . . . *v*

Introduction *1*

I   Love Yourself. 7

II   Love All Human Beings 19

III Love All Living Creatures 37

IV Love Your Creator. 47

V   Love Your Planet Earth. 59

VI Love Your Gift of Life and Death 69

VII Love Your Work 89

VIII Love Your Place of Residence 105

IX Love Your Experiences 121

X   Love Your Moment of Being 133

Conclusion. *147*

About the Author. *157*

Index *159*

Introduction

*A*waken, dear ones of planet Earth. Awaken and remember who we truly are. We are loving, spiritual beings temporarily in a physical body. We are created in the image of God and are part of the divine whole in God's divine plan.

Our purpose here on planet Earth is solely for our souls' evolvement. We chose planet Earth because we felt it was one of the best schools in the universe to experience who we are or who we are not. By the free will God has given us, we play out countless scenes in the creation of our lives.

We have chosen to incarnate upon this planet lifetime after lifetime until we experience and live our lives as the masters did and still do. The answer is, and always has been, made simple and easy for us to understand. God simply wants us to love each other as he has loved us. Written ideals and those applied to actual experiences are not the same. That's why we are here—to learn to incorporate God's simple message in every aspect of our lives.

Every circumstance, condition and obstacle in our lives are created or uncreated by us, by the power God has given us. Therefore, God is not responsible for the outcome of our lives. God created us and has given us free choice to do as we wish. We create our lives and times by our own thought forms, for the words we think and speak will manifest themselves in our physical reality.

Individual thought forms are very real, and can be seen within other dimensions. Because like attracts like, positive thoughts gather together, as do negative thought forms. In reality, we are all collectively creating together. Our thoughts directly affect our lives, the lives of others and all people on planet Earth. This means we have a direct influence on the future of our planet.

Our souls understand only two emotions: the emotion of love or its opposite, fear. When dealing with ourselves and our relationships, making decisions in our homes and workplaces, educating our children or when engaging in the politics of war and peace or the uniting and dividing people, will we choose thoughts of love or thoughts of fear? The choice is ours.

We must monitor our thinking. Any time we have hateful thoughts about someone, we can cancel those thoughts by visualizing a big "X" over them. Practice positive thinking. Life can be either difficult or easy, as we so choose.

God does not judge us for the way we choose to live our lives. God does not punish us for doing things

we consider wrong. We were given free will, and therefore we can access how well we're doing or have done.
There are neither right nor wrong answers to the
choices we make. Our choices to live our lives in either
love or fear tells us who we are, what we are about and
what our souls evolvement is at any moment.

What would happen if most people on this planet
would choose to live their lives in love, think loving
thoughts, speak loving words and act in loving ways?
Truly unconditional love can move mountains, reach
the darkest corners, travel great distances and bring us
back to the Garden of Eden. Is it really difficult to love
each other? By being here at this moment, we all have a
chance to change the predictions of our prophets, both
past and present. I dare us to become a new race of
beings, one that is self-realized and highly evolved. The
choice is ours.

I hope you enjoy *The Ten Commitments of Love* on the
following pages. Read each one and then reread each
one again. Try to integrate these simple messages into
action in your lives. The messages are illuminators.
Listen for what resonates with your being. Go within
and listen to your higher self; listen to the songs of
angels; listen to the God within. Only then will you
find your truth within, where the truth resides and
always will be.

I invite you to join me in awakening people on this
beloved planet we call Earth. Equipped with faith,
hope and love, we have the power to open the hearts
and minds of all beings.

Become a messenger as I am and help spread the word of *The Ten Commitments of Love*. Pass this journal to loved ones, family members, friends, neighbors and co-workers, until people finally understand God's simple message. God and the great masters have been trying to present these simple messages for eons. This is simply a journal for living life on planet Earth. Do not leave home without it.

I

Love Yourself

Love Yourself

*L*ove yourself unconditionally with all your heart, mind and soul, as the Creator has loved you. To love yourself unconditionally means to place no conditions on yourself. Give yourself a break and don't be so hard on yourself. Your purpose here at this time is to help spread the word of love to every person who crosses your path. Your soul is not concerned about competing in this world. Your soul understands that competition only separates the human race. Who invented the word *competition*? It's about time you erase that word from your mind's dictionary and from the education of your children.

Competition correlates to fear—specifically, fear of not reaching the top and fear that others will get more than we have. We compete to obtain better jobs, vehicles and homes. If we are successful, we purchase larger homes and more expensive vehicles and furnishings. We strive to have the best of everything, but even then, we fear that we will lose our possessions. In order to protect them, we install expensive security systems and buy insurance policies. Some people even have prenuptial agreements drawn up to protect their prized material possessions from a loved one.

Shortly after we're dead some relatives may argue over what they think they're entitled to. They fear someone in the family might receive more than they do. Fear spreads like wildfire. It causes family jealousies and hard feelings.

I use the word *possessions* in particular to suggest how our material wealth actually possesses *us*. We acquire high mortgage payments, credit card bills and vehicle payments and then we ponder what happened to us as we try to make those payments. We need to understand the power of the competitiveness we ourselves have created. We need to understand how it can cause so much fear, separation and chaos in our lives and in the lives of others.

Awaken, dear ones, and uncreate competition. Start with the children and teach them that it's okay not to be at the "top." Every being is different and grows and evolves when his or her soul is ready, not when a parent or teacher is ready. Let's not have our new race of children compete for the highest grades or to be the fastest in sports. By encouraging competition, we instill fear in them when they do not live up to our expectations or to the expectations of their teachers and coaches.

Allow each soul to grow and learn at its own

pace. Praise all children for their efforts, not the results. Stop comparing them to other children and view them as individual souls who are walking their own paths. It's about time for us to review ourselves as parents and to review our school systems. We need to choose a higher path for teaching our children. We need to erase or cancel competition from our lives and the lives of our children.

Remember that we create or uncreate by the power God has given us. We can create or uncreate the lessons we teach at home and the agendas of our school system. To teach these young souls, will we choose lessons derived from fear or love? Have we not remembered and learned from our own childhood memories? The choice is ours.

Fear causes people to resist change. Many of us fear losing our positions in the community by standing up for what we believe. Some people have to compete to reach these higher positions; others achieve a higher standing because of whom they know. Still others step on people to achieve their goals.

Some people fear change itself, and don't want to try something new. But we can all write new agendas—agendas that lead our children as well as ourselves to our higher selves. What a wondrous new path to choose! And by choosing with love, the path before us is illuminated in a glorious new way. When actions are taken with love, future paths will always be filled with wonderful opportunities for growth for our own souls and the souls of our children. The teaching of our children is placed in our hands, and it is up to us to decide what these teachings will be.

When we love ourselves unconditionally, we do not place judgments on ourselves. Let's stop comparing ourselves to other people. Each of us who travels through this wonderful journey called life is unique.

There is no one like you because you are a one-of-a-kind soul. Remember that there are no such things as right or wrong answers on the path of life. God does not punish you if you "messed up." You are the only one who can reflect on how you're doing and decide if you can do better. How you react to situations in life tells you who you are and it tells you about the condition of your soul's evolvement at a given time.

If you do not like the way your life is going, change direction. Choose another path. It's as simple as that. You can choose how to handle each experience you encounter. Your encounters can be experienced in love or fear.

To love yourself unconditionally means to be lighter with life. Don't always be so serious. There is a purpose for every person on this planet. Learn to accept yourself as a unique individual, but don't look at yourself as better or lower than others. Each person is created equal. Some wealthy people forget this and think that poor people are of less value than they are. This is not true, for all God's children are created equal and deserving of his great abundance.

When we finally understand the laws of God and the universe, no human being will ever be without. By thinking we will never have abundance, we create just that. When we buy into the negative thinking of the end of the world, we create what we don't want. We are very powerful beings, but we forget our power and who we truly are.

As we entered into our Earth bodies, we relinquished our memories of ourselves so that we could experience our Earth lessons. When we remember who we truly are, we will embrace ourselves in total love and joy.

I say to you now, awaken, dear ones, and remember who you are. You are a spiritual being who is temporarily in a physical body. As you learn lesson after lesson, you are evolving and moving closer to God. Your lessons can be as difficult or as easy as you choose them to be. You can learn your lessons in this lifetime, or continue to learn in future lifetimes until you get them. Every action you undertake in this lifetime has both cause and effect. Will you nudge other people toward love or fear?

To become a master of yourself means to love yourself unconditionally. Place no judgments on yourself. Accept yourself for who you are, and if you don't like who you are, create a new you.

To love yourself unconditionally means to forgive yourself for any negative words you've spoken to yourself. There is no such thing as being perfect.

When you use the word *perfect*, You judge either others or yourself for being less than perfect. Let he who is without fault cast the first stone.

Your soul does not understand "perfect," nor is it concerned about perfection because it knows that after it has experienced one lesson, there will always be another to experience. You are constantly attending school, even in your dream state. While dreaming, your soul travels and attends classes within the astral world. These classes can be within other galaxies, universes, planets or star systems.

All God's children are created equal. Just because some people either have physical disabilities or appear less intelligent than us, they are not necessarily less important or less perfect than we are. As a matter of fact, when we spend a few moments with a disabled person, we soon realize that they are very much evolved beings. Maybe we can all learn something from them.

When we created the word *disability*, we meant that certain people did not have certain abilities. We did not mean that they have no purpose here. Some disabled people think that they do not have a disability at all. Well, glory be in the highest, they have learned how to apply the power of thought. Learn from these dear souls, for they have many lessons to teach us.

It's never too late to love yourself. Remember that you are here for a purpose. That purpose can be as simple as learning to love yourself unconditionally or to help others awaken and remember who they are. Life does not have to be difficult. The choice is and always will be yours.

Next time you get angry with yourself for doing something you considered stupid, think again. Instead, laugh at yourself, roll on the ground in laughter and make funny noises and funny faces. Can you imagine your neighbors seeing you roll around laughing on your front lawn? They might think you're nuts, but they will watch you anyway. Tell them it's a new way of releasing stress. You might be surprised at how many people join you. You have no one to impress and no one to prove anything to. You don't need other's opinions to help you shape the decisions you make in your life. You are a very self-sufficient being and are capable of making your own decisions.

Have you ever become excited about something that you did and not been able to wait to share it with other people? Later, however, when you told other people, they weren't always as excited as you were or they told you something negative about what you had just done. You lost that excitement and wondered if it was as good an idea as you once thought it was. Sometimes it is best to keep things to yourself. When you truly realize this, you will know that you do not need other people's approval.

Your joy is within. It is sometimes best shared only with your inner friend because that inner friend will support you in whatever decision you make. If you feel you made a "mistake," you can discuss it with that inner friend, who is yourself. By taking this approach, no other person can take your energy from you by means of his or her negative opinions, nor can they tell you, "I told you so" later.

To love yourself means to treat yourself with respect. Don't be afraid to talk to yourself. You are your best companion, so pat yourself on your back once in a while. Give yourself credit for your efforts, whatever the outcome. Your efforts tell you who you are and what you're about. Your soul is not concerned with outcomes. What counts is the effort you put into an experience. Outcomes only tell you if you're happy with that experience or if you could have done better.

Although some experiences may have been difficult, once you learn to love yourself, the difficult experiences seem to subside and you attract happier events in your life. What you put out is what you're going to receive. Stop feeling sorry for yourself and get back on the horse. Learn the power of love because with love all things are possible. Don't get too wrapped up in the material world, but instead concentrate on your spiritual growth. Your spiritual growth is what counts, because when you evolve spiritually, your evolutionary soul evolves also.

To love yourself with all your heart and soul is the wisest and most rewarding path to choose. Try putting these simple lessons into action and you will witness firsthand the true magic of love.

To love yourself does not mean to place expectations on yourself. Learn to give it your all, and that's it. If that's the best you can do in the moment, you will know. Don't place others' limitations or expectations on yourself. Every person has the power to create or uncreate himself at will. Have the will and inspiration to change if you choose to do so. If you're happy with who you are and are doing the best you can do, that's what matters.

I wrote this book to give you, the reader, a choice to be who you are. By following God's simple messages in this book, you have an opportunity to evolve as fast or as slow as you choose. Take from these lessons what you feel you can live with, and then live them. It's as simple as that.

When you live God's simple lessons, you will experience wonderful occurrences in your life. When you start with loving yourself, all other commitments magically fall into place. I use the word *commitments* instead of *commandments* because you are committing to loving yourself—not commanding yourself. To commit to yourself is the wisest gift you can give yourself.

Other people will feel attracted to your love vibration. Loving yourself sets up a beacon of love and light energy that surrounds your entire being and then catapults out into the universe. This signal draws to its source or you, like minds, which is people who love themselves.

The masters and angels have been watching

closely over us. They know our trials and tribulations. They know how far some of us have traveled. They're waiting patiently to rejoice in a new world of beings and a return of the utopia we once had. Let's have it again. A choice to have our Garden of Eden can be made in a holy instant. The choice is ours. If we all practice these lessons, we will be on our way toward mastering life on the physical level.

Love All
Human Beings

Love All Human Beings

L ove all human beings unconditionally. This
means accept everyone for who they are in the
moment of their being. When we learn to love ourselves unconditionally, loving other people comes
naturally. This is where some people seem to have a
hard time, and this is why planet Earth is in the
shape it's in now. Until we all understand this and
live it, how can we evolve into a new race of beings?

Dear ones, please understand that to love others
as God has loved you is not as hard as you think. I
say to you now, awaken and remember who you are.
You truly are a loving spiritual being. Everyone on
this planet now is at a different level of evolvement.

Even people who kill, rape, steal and abuse other
people are at different levels of evolvement. They
don't understand the laws of cause and effect. These
poor souls neither love themselves nor others
because if they did, they would not be committing

these violent acts. I say "poor souls" because they
have forgotten who they are, and this alone is a great
tragedy. They are lost in a world of their own fear,
unaware that God exists.

When we succumb to fear in terms of our thinking and speech and actions, we are lead into the
darkest corners of every aspect of our lives. Fear contains jealousy, anger, rage and blame. It can make us
disrespectful, judgmental, resentful and blind and
deaf to love.

There is not one person who escapes the universal
laws of God. There is no place to hide and no place to
run. God does not judge us, nor can any judge or jury.
We have only ourselves to assess how well we're
doing. What will happen to these poor souls? The law
of cause and effect is real and active and if these souls
don't learn to love themselves and other people in
this lifetime, they will have to return and repeat lifetime after lifetime until they experience love.

Upon their death, these souls will have to account
for any negative actions that took place while they
were in their Earth bodies. They will receive a review
of their lives and feel the pain and suffering they
have inflicted on themselves and others. They will
witness the ripple effect from the families and lives
they touched by their negative actions. No jail time
can ever compare to the assessment of one's life that
occurs after death.

These lost souls, spiritual beings in Earth bodies,
chose Earth as a place in which to experience and

evolve. Like us, those souls relinquished their memories of themselves for the purpose of evolvement. Upon entering this physical environment, they were equipped with lessons they needed to learn for their souls' growth. These souls as pure spirit never intended to come to the Earth plane to kill, rape and harm other people. By being children of God or part of God, they did not know of such behaviors while they were in spirit form.

Upon encountering their life lessons, these souls had a choice as to how they were going to experience them. There are only two choices that our souls understand—love or fear. Lost souls too often choose to experience fear and all the attributes that fear embodies. The real tragedy is that some of them don't remember who they are until it's too late.

Sometimes when these souls return into the dimension of spirit, they are confused and can't seem to find the light because they are blinded by their own negative thought forms. Some people may think of this as hell, but there is no such place. We are the ones who created that idea, not God. However, I assure you that for lost souls being stuck on that dense, dark plane is a living hell.

If and when these souls find the light, their spirit guides help them. Suddenly they awaken, and within the light they see the effects of their negative actions. These poor souls now understand that since they did not experience their lessons in loving ways, they will have to return to the Earth plane again, but on their next trip they will have extra baggage filled with negative karma from the previous life. People who think they're untouchable and can get away with all kinds of negative actions, should think again. In their next lives, people will treat them the way they treated others. This is all because they chose to experience their previous lives in fear instead of love.

Remember that God gave us free will to choose who we are and who we are not. When we choose love, it is always the wisest path to God and our ticket home. God hears, sees and knows our most sincere desires and whether they are really from the heart or not. Some people think they are fooling others but when it is their time, they will have to assess how well they have done. Sometimes these poor souls have difficulty forgiving themselves and need time in the spirit world to recuperate from the Earth plane.

God wants us to come home and join him in his kingdom of heaven, but until we think, speak and live love in our lives, we will have to repeat these incarnations on the Earth plane over and over.

To love others unconditionally means to pass no judgment on them. Each soul has a purpose and is evolving according to its level of being. You will know your level of being the next time you hear about a violent act. What will your reaction be? Will you react out of love or out of fear? Will you buy into the reactions of others? What effect will the newspapers, television and media have on you? Will you contribute to the negative thought forms that encompass all acts of violence, or will you add light and love?

To love others unconditionally means to be non-judgmental. As hard as it may seem to us, some of us have brought negative actions to others in past lives even though we have now learned and evolved into the souls we are today. Think about that. Do we really know how many times we had to return to the Earth plane? We can only send loving thoughts and prayers to these lost souls so that someday they too will remember who they are.

To love other's unconditionally means to forgive others for any wrongdoing they have done to you. Remember who they are and who you are. Some people hold grudges for many years and don't get to mend relationships until it's too late. Some people have a hard time forgiving and forgetting what other people may have done to them. If you do not mend a relationship now, you will have to mend it in the next lifetime, until the energies between you are balanced. Don't you think it's easier to mend it now rather than carry it with you into another lifetime?

There's no escaping karmic debt. If you can't get in touch with a person, then mentally open your heart and send love whether you feel you were right or wrong in your actions toward him. The acts of forgiveness and sending love could mend the deepest of wounds and set you free to continue moving forward in the evolution of your soul.

People are led into your life by the universal law of attraction. The lesson you need to learn can be as simple as forgiveness. Your soul knows what lessons it needs to learn in this lifetime. You attract people and situations for the purpose of experiencing lessons. Your own higher self leads these people to you. They are gifts for you. Appreciate these people for coming into your life, no matter how hard the experience was in the end. If you chose to experience the lesson of love, then congratulations—you have just evolved to another level of being.

When people don't want to forgive others, they hold themselves back from their own growth. They will continue to draw others to them who can teach them that lesson, until they have mastered it.

Realize that each person is a unique being besides differences in appearance, style, race, creed and sexual preference. Before incarnating on the Earth plane, we each chose a race, gender and sexual preference. Our souls knew they would be greatly challenged and have lessons to learn, especially as a minority within the Earth plane. By the way, who invented the word *minority*? Who really is a *minority*? God's answer to that is that none of us are. We created that idea, too.

When we are in pure spirit form, we are neither male, female, black, white, yellow, red or green. We are all simply the same. The only difference is our vibrational level. Each soul vibrates at a different level according to its growth.

If you are a loving person, you will be able to hold more light and therefore vibrate in higher dimensions. If you are hateful and unforgiving, you will hold less light and therefore vibrate in the lower dimensions. Your level of being can be changed at any time by thought, speech and action. Souls in the spirit world recognize other souls by their vibrations or light.

Can you imagine the shock to our young souls when people prejudge them? Who created the word *prejudice*? It's about time we erase this word from our mind's dictionary and cast it off planet Earth forever.

When people are prejudiced, they do not love other people unconditionally. What is with this black, white and gay thing? Who cares what others are. When God said to love everyone, he meant everyone. How are people really different? All humans cry, laugh, eat, sleep and have feelings, too. The problem is that too many people see only the outside, which is the physical vehicle and not the true spiritual person inside. People who are prejudiced in this world must have forgotten who they are, or they would not have the word *prejudice* in their vocabulary.

Fear causes prejudice. Prejudiced people are afraid of beings who are different than they are. Should we expect everyone to look like us? Prejudice causes separateness within the human race. It is about time that we stop being self-centered about whom we think should exist on this planet. The planet is on loan to us for the purpose of our soul's growth. We do not own the ground we walk on, nor do we have a say in who

can walk on it. There will always be black, white,
yellow, red, green and gay people living on this
planet. The only reason we are called black, white,
yellow, red, green or gay is because we created those
distinctions. We gave meaning to those words to separate from each other. Why not call everyone people or
human beings? Is this not what we are?

True unconditional love for all human beings
means to accept all people for who they are. Place no
judgment upon them and respect them all as your
brothers and sisters because, in reality, they are.

Life is too short to ponder over which colors we
like best in a rainbow or which color we don't like at
all. See the beauty and wonderment of it all!
Wouldn't life be boring if everyone were the same?
What if we all had the same face, eyes, nose, hair and
body? God created us different so we wouldn't go
stir-crazy staring at ourselves. How would you like
to date someone who looked like all the other people
you dated? Wow, what a scary concept!

Who are gay people? They are people who happen
to enjoy and love the same gender. That's it, nothing
else. They are not perverted people waiting to grab us
from behind a bush. They have better things to do
with their lives. People who are prejudiced against
gay people have to work on their fears because if they
were not prejudiced, their fear would not exist.

No person on this planet can influence another
person without that person's allowing it. If we, or
our children, associate with someone who is gay,

we won't become gay unless we choose to be.

Some people think that gay people are the only ones who have AIDS or that we can only contract AIDS from a gay person. This is far from the truth. We need to seek out true knowledge and not accept information passed on by gossip. How do we know that information is not distorted by the time it reaches us? Anyone who uses unsafe practices can contract this disease. No one is beyond its reach.

To love others unconditionally means to have a relationship of nonattachment. When you're in a relationship with someone, know that your higher selves brought you together. You are meant to learn something from each other. Lessons can be as simple as patience, understanding or compassion, or as difficult as rejection. Lessons are as difficult or as easy as you choose. Before you were born, your soul knew what it needed to experience in order to evolve.

To love yourself unconditionally means that you don't need to seek happiness from other people. When you're seeking or expecting others to make you happy, eventually you will be disappointed. By having an attitude of nonattachment toward others, you will never be disappointed because you understand there is a reason why this person has come into your life or left it.

A healthy relationship involves people who first love themselves. They understand that they can love the other person to the extent they can love themselves unconditionally. They can give each other love, support, compassion and encouragement as long as they do not include competition, jealousy or judgment. They can learn and grow together independent of each other—that to say, in a relationship of nonattachment. They can stay together as long as they continue to guide each other to their higher selves, but they are not attached to the outcome. This is truly a match made in heaven and it is available to all of us. When we love ourselves unconditionally, people who are compatible with our energies are magically drawn to our love vibrations.

Some relationships come and go like the wind whereas others last a lifetime. Relationships change because one person grows at a different rate than the other. This is neither right nor wrong. As people experience and learn, they change and evolve. At some point one or both people may become unhappy or restless, experience anxiety, appear lazy and are not be sure why. When this occurs, the two people need to sit down and talk. If it's meant for their souls to stay together, they will work it out. They will know and feel the answer within.

If people would only communicate their feelings at this point instead of having an affair, which causes so much unnecessary pain for others. By talking over their feelings, two people will either work it out or separate, so that both individuals are free to move forward with their lives.

Some people like to have their cake and eat it too. This approach is selfish, unloving and disrespectful to the other person. If one feels a need to get involved with a new person while currently in a relationship, one should sever the old relationship first, so that person can move forward with his life. People who think they are fooling their mates are in reality fooling themselves.

The previous paragraph needed to be written because cheating occurs every day all over the world. If you love yourself and others unconditionally, cheating cannot be in your vocabulary because you understand that you would only be cheating yourself.

Remember the universal laws of cause and effect: Every action we take is accounted for. When one causes grief to others, one too will experience the ripple effect as well as the grief. When we understand the above principles and apply it in our lives, we will have helped not only ourselves, but also the human race as a whole. Resisting the temptation to cheat is sometimes the hardest lesson to learn, and it comes from fear. When we overcome our temptations, fear vanishes with the wind and love is free to take the reins.

People who don't love themselves unconditionally have a hard time meeting the right person or holding onto relationships. That is because their vibrations attract people who also don't love themselves. Next time you wonder why your relationships never work out, review chapter one and integrate it into your life. It's okay to read inspirational writings, but until you put them to work in your life, they are only words on a page. Knowledge or wisdom taken from a book is helpful to the extent that you experience it. Your soul is here to experience lessons, not read about them.

People who don't love themselves in a relationship often seem to thrive on fear rather than love. Fear of being alone or starting over, the weight of a long-term relationship, the fear of not finding anyone else: all are reasons used for staying in relationships that aren't working. Fear causes a lack of trust. It creates doubt, suspicion and worry that the other person is being unfaithful. Fear ripples outward, taking with it everything in its path. Giving in to fear is to feel what it's like at the bottom of a dark cage. There seems to be no escape until you start to see a faint light at the end of the tunnel. That light is called love, and that experience is called evolvement.

By following God's simple law of unconditional love for self and others, your life will be more of a joy than a struggle. Why do some people stay in mentally or physically abusive relationships? The answer is clear: They choose them. They choose to experience their lives in fear instead of love. These souls neither love nor respect themselves because, if they did, they would not allow another being to treat them in such a way.

People in this type of relationship have an important lesson to learn—to love themselves with all their heart and soul. They will then feel the veils of fear lift gently and see a new path as the door of hope opens. God hears their cries and sees their sufferings but will not interfere with their free will and the choices they make.

God patiently waits for these people to open their hearts and minds to a much brighter path filled with joy and happiness. This path was always there and will always be waiting for them. The path is called love. When they decide to reach out and choose this path, people will mysteriously appear, taking their hands and gently guiding them through. People who care about these lost souls see their sufferings and feel their pain but it is up to the person himself to stay or leave.

By choosing to stay, they are not helping the abusers because abusers cannot love themselves or anyone else. Abusers live in a world of fear and try to control and manipulate everyone around them. They thrive on the fear of others, and that fear makes them stronger and others weaker. They steal energy from others.

People who are abused appear tired and seem to have no spirit left, because they have given their energy to the abuser, either consciously or unconsciously. People who abuse others have no respect for themselves or anyone else and they continue to grow stronger as long as others remain afraid.

If abusers do not choose to seek help and find the path of love, this cycle will continue until they destroy everything around them including their own dreams. This is a sad thing for these souls because they choose darkness instead of light and sadness instead of happiness and fear instead of love. I emphasize the word *choose* because they can *choose* to abuse or not.

When people choose to stay in abusive relationships, the abusers will continue to tell them that they can't live without them, the abusers. What they are really saying is that *they*, the abusers, cannot live without their victims, because there would be no one left to abuse but themselves. Remember that if victims choose to stay, they must not blame God or their abusers. We all have free will about how we want to experience our lives. True unconditional love for others means knowing when to stay or leave. If you are unhappy, you already know the answer within yourself.

As difficult as it may seem, bless your abusers, for they have shown you who you are and who you are not. However painful, forgive them silently for their wrongdoings. Send them love and light as you walk out the door so that someday they too might awaken and remember who they are. Their coming into your life has made you more aware of the power of fear and the power of love. If the abusers don't change in this lifetime, after death they will have to review their lives and feel the pain and suffering they have inflicted on others.

Loving yourself will always give you the courage and strength to move forward. Loving others will allow you to accept all people for who they are at any moment.

Angels are patiently waiting to take the hand of all abused persons and guide them to a much brighter path. Seek the path of love, and you will find more joy, happiness, laughter and peace than you ever thought existed. Practice these lessons, and you will find happiness beyond your wildest dreams.

Love All
Living Creatures

Love All Living Creatures

ove all living creatures with all your heart and
soul. Respect the animal kingdom, and they in
turn will respect you. God placed animals as well as
humans on planet Earth for a purpose. Mother
Nature is the keeper of the animal kingdom, feeding
them and giving them a place to live.

Animals are created equal to humans, which
means that we have no authority over animals even
though some of us think we have. Who created the
idea of authority? No one has authority over any
other person or living creature. We have no right to
cage animals and hold them against their free will.
Humans do not have to view animals in a cage for
selfish pleasure or profit, nor do we need to use them
for medical research. God did not place these wonderful creatures on this planet for those reasons.

We have the power to tap into the human mind
by means of the gifts God has bestowed on us. Why

do diseases such as cancer, AIDS and heart disease exist? Diseases are never a plague from God. *We* create them all. Our negative thinking and lack of self-love have manifested these diseases in the physical world.

Negative thinking has a tremendous impact on our mental, emotional and physical states. Our cells and physical structure respond to what we think of ourselves. Hate, for example, has the power to change even the healthiest cells into unhealthy ones. What we think, so shall we be.

The solutions have been and always will be within. When you experience unconditional love, you will be able to access solutions to difficult problems. Why do many diseases not exist in certain countries where some people live well past one hundred years of age? The answer is: These people practice respect and love of self, others and all living creatures.

These healthier people grow their foods in organic soil free from chemicals. They consume foods filled with vitamins and minerals. They exercise daily and meditate under the stars at night. They take care of and respect their animals and feed them the same quality of food as they eat themselves. They know that to feed them anything less would only hurt themselves. Such people consume only what they need. They don't need a head of an animal on the wall for display or to satisfy their egos. Other people like to brag about how many animals they've killed and how many heads they've mounted on their walls. I suggest that these people buy pictures of animals instead.

People in these countries have no need for money to sustain themselves, but instead exchange, trade or share what little they have. I say "little" because some of us think that what they have indicates poverty, but in reality they are rich in health, mind and spirit. Simplicity in life is perhaps one of the keys we've been searching for. The word *simple* means not complicated.

Such people understand love, kindness, compassion, joy and laughter and they care for their neighbors. They know if they didn't, they would only be hurting themselves because there wouldn't be anyone to trade with or laugh with. You never know when you might need your neighbors in an emergency. They could save your life.

When these people meditate or pray daily, there is no room for negative thinking. This keeps their minds and bodies free of major diseases. If and when they fall ill, they turn to nature for fresh, soothing herbs. Stress does not exist, because there's no rush hour or mortgages to pay. They build their homes with the help of others as a mutual exchange. What would they need money for? No wonder these people live healthy, happy and prosperous lives free of major disease.

We have learned to rely on greedy corporations for our food, which is far from healthy, full of dangerous chemicals and additives and unfit for human consumption. Our animals are injected with steroids and other growth-altering chemicals. The bigger the animal, the larger the profit. But what happens to us when we eat those animals?

Do you think the only reason vegetarians don't eat meat is because they are animal activists? No, they understand that meat slows down their energy level and affects their vibrational level. Did you ever eat red meat and feel tired shortly after? Other countries around the world understand this, and that's why they eat grains, beans, vegetables and fruits. They understand that red meat prevents them from achieving higher vibrational frequencies.

If you understand this, you have an opportunity to think for yourself and lead a healthier life. Don't take my word for it. Do your own research. Learn to read labels. If you can't pronounce the ingredients or understand them, that product is probably not natural, which means it's not entirely produced from nature.

Most canned foods in stores contain preservatives and additives to maintain shelf life. Some of us buy these canned products out of laziness, and because they are less expensive. They are convenient because of our busy schedules. This has been a common way of thinking for many years.

Convenience foods are just that. They are convenient for our wallets and busy schedules, but not for our health and doctor bills. The main concern of most growers today is to pump out as much produce

as possible, and adding chemicals is the fastest way
to achieve that goal. Although I have a hard time
calling that food, we're still buying it, so they still
produce it.

Some companies squeeze animals into tight quar-
ters so they are almost on top of each other. No
wonder these animals are depressed and angry. Just
think of all the negative feelings these animals have
and then we eat them, feelings and all. We don't
have to be animal activists or have much intelligence
to see this as cruel and inhumane treatment, which
produces meat that is dangerous for human consumption, and totally against God's laws. I would
not want to be the souls responsible for these actions
especially when it is life-review time.

When does this cruelty end? When we choose. It's
as simple as that. By the power God has given us, we
can move mountains or fly to the moon. What makes
us think we're not capable of shutting down these
negative food sources?

When we truly learn the meaning of unconditional love for self, others and all living creatures,
we will stop buying these negative products.
Instead, we will turn to organic produce and meat
or grow our own food. Whatever path we choose,
if we choose it in love, the answer has already
been written. When we realize that these greedy
companies no longer serve us, we will have
evolved to a higher level of being. When we are
filled with love, then disease and fear cannot exist.

Organic farmers do not use harmful chemicals for their produce or inject their animals with unnatural substances. They do not cram their animals in tight boxes or stack them on top of each other. They feed their families and neighbors organic foods. They do this because they care for themselves and all other beings. Their animals are happy and not stressed, and in return they give back healthy foods to consume. Even though red meat lowers one's vibration level, consuming organic meats is much healthier than its counterpart.

I think organic farmers are sound of mind and spirit. Organic foods are becoming more and more popular in today's food markets. Some people complain that organic food prices are costlier than chemical-laden foods, but can we place a price tag on our health? My grandmother Florence once said from her hospital bed, "Michele, if you don't have your health, all the money you saved over the years means nothing." I watched her and others like her suffer from terrible diseases. I believe her negative thinking caused some of it, but chemically-treated foods also played a part.

Animals as well as humans were born to be free. Perhaps some animals are more evolved than some humans—you don't see them trying to place us in a cage. To love yourself and all others means to allow each being to be who it is, without interfering with God's divine plan. Haven't these poor creatures suffered enough? Maybe the people responsible for harming them will have to return to the Earth plane as animals in their next lifetimes.

There are no more words that can be written about this subject. How many more books, articles, posters and media sources do we need to understand this simple message that God has been telling us? The next time we see an animal chained in a yard for endless hours or days, perhaps we should ask ourselves how the animal is feeling.

A jail cell for a human being is no different then a chain around a tree for a dog. Both environments are restrictive. Animals don't commit crimes. Therefore, they don't deserve the chain to the tree. Unless we try chaining ourselves to a tree all day or all week, we cannot possibly know how they feel. Love for self, others and all living creatures are the only keys to God's kingdom.

IV

Love Your Creator

Love Your Creator

L ove your Creator unconditionally with all your
heart, mind and soul. There is only one God
who is responsible for creating all that is. God created life itself upon this planet, other planets, this
universe and other universes in a holy instant.
Human beings are a ray of God, children of God;
therefore people are all a spark of the divine Creator.

God is everywhere, in everything and in every
person twenty-four hours a day. Loving yourself and
all others is the same as loving God, because God
resides in all that is. Place no other gods before him.
Be grateful to God for all he has given you for the
purpose of your soul's evolution.

There are no right or wrong religions to follow
as long as they lead to God. The problem with some
religions is that they think their way is the only
correct one to follow. Some religions say that if you
don't follow their way, you will go to hell or God

will punish you in some way. These statements are far from the truth and deceive the people on this planet. After being made fearful, no wonder that some choose not to attend religious services.

God does not punish us if we choose not to attend church or a religious function. God wants us to awaken and remember who we are and love each other without judgment. If we choose to awaken and love others at either a church or in our homes, it is our choice, not to be judged by others. It's a matter of choosing where we want to speak to God.

Some people attend church to pray to God, while others pray in their homes or outdoors in nature. Neither path is right or wrong. It's a matter of personal choice. God will speak to us wherever we are. We don't have to travel great distances, look up to the heavens or wait till death to communicate with God. We will know and feel God when we open our hearts and minds.

Close your eyes and feel His presence in every cell of your body. One of the ways God speaks to you is through your intuition. When you learn to follow your intuition, it is God and your higher self speaking to you. If the experience leads you to a higher path, you will know the path is a true one. God speaks with you through your heart. When your heart is open, the doorway to God is open.

Run from any religion that tries to convince you that their way is the only way. To love others unconditionally means not to judge others because of their religion or lack of it. Allow each soul to walk its own path and not necessarily yours. No group has the right to brainwash others into thinking their religion is the only one without suffering karmic consequences.

Some ministers and priests practice what they preach about loving others, whereas others merely deliver a good speech. Until they experience loving others, their words will remain a set of ideas formed on a sheet of paper. Will they choose words that generate love or fear? When such preachers awaken and remember who they are, they will teach only of one highest good for all human beings. They will teach people to have unconditional love for self and all others. They will cast their staff on planet Earth and guide rather than lead or command. People will find themselves when they are ready, and only then will they find God.

There are various religious cultures because there are different people on this planet. If you have a desire to follow a certain religion, do so no matter what religion you were raised with. A true house of God is open to all who enter.

Many names are used for the Creator, but there is only one Creator of all that is. Whatever name you choose or whatever house you pray in, know that there is only one God, or Creator, the I Am That I Am. You shall place no other gods before him because God is all that is.

There is no right or wrong way to speak to God. Remember that God hears, sees and touches every part of our lives and is in all beings. The only difference is that some people choose to tune in to God while others shut off the radio. We are all God's children, and he wants us all to evolve so we can return home.

Did you ever feel like you don't belong or fit in? That's because your soul wants to return to its spiritual home but it knows it needs to experience its lessons and master life at the physical level first. That's it. Sounds simple, but most people have a hard time hearing and living with this simple message of unconditional love.

I use the word *him* throughout this book to refer to God, even though God is both male and female. Some speak of him as Father/Mother God. God is all that is; therefore, God is all that exists. To think of God as only one sex is to limit our thinking. God has no limits, only we do. We limit our thinking in many things because of fear. Limitations and fear hold us back while no limits and love help us expand.

Some people spend their lives running from God because their religions tell them they won't go to heaven if they don't attend church. The real tragedy is that some of these souls are children, and when children learn to fear God at an early age, they carry that memory into adulthood. Preaching such a message is both destructive and untrue. These children/adults acquire a fear of God and later question what and who God is. Some even deny God or doubt his existence in reaction to the teachings, which violate their sense of justice.

Children are very vulnerable and what they are taught is stored deep within their subconscious minds for their lifetime, affecting them unconsciously. Preachers should reevaluate what they are teaching, because they will someday experience the ripple effect of their untruthful words and actions. A true preacher of God is a messenger of the highest good and is committed to tell the truth to all who listen. Such a messenger is a channel of God's word and his message has nothing to do with a preacher's ego or lower self.

If God were a judging God, then why would he give us free will to choose our experiences and learn from our mistakes? A gift is a gift and is not to be taken back. If God were a judging God, he would have to separate the so-called good from the bad. And if that were the case, we all would be punished because we all have made mistakes. But, neither the universe nor God operates judgmentally.

God gave us free choice and opportunities to find our way back home to him. God does not punish us for taking the wrong path. We are the only ones who can find the path that will lead to him. We call these paths our experiences and we call our experiences lessons. If God gave us all the keys to life or to our own pathways, would we need to be here?

The secret to the universe is that there *is* no secret! God designed life and made it simple for us. There are no hidden secrets. We all have the knowledge of life and how the universe works stored deep within

our subconscious minds. When we go within to
retrieve that knowledge, we will all find the same
answer—which is for us to love each other. It's as
simple as that.

Did Jesus not mess up in his past lives? Jesus
learned many of life's lessons from his past incarnations, but he also learned to experience love of self,
of others and of all living creatures and offered his
services to the world without judgment.

Jesus performed miracles because he did not limit
himself and had no doubt about his healing abilities.
He trusted and had faith in God and thereby
acknowledged God in advance for any miracle that
would take place. Did Jesus not say, "What I can do,
ye can do greater"? We too are gifted with the power
of healing, but we limit our thinking and believe
only "great ones" can perform such acts. If Jesus had
limited his thinking or had had doubts about his
abilities, would he have been able to perform those
healings? Jesus understood the power of thought and
how to manipulate matter. We too have this gift, but
we have limited our thinking for so many years that
we have now forgotten who we are and what we are
capable of.

People who perform miracles today have remembered who they are and have put into action those
gifts that God has bestowed on every one. Do not
allow another person to tell you that you can't do
something, or that you will not be able to understand
a certain book or be able to perform a healing such as

Jesus did. They are only trying to obscure the truth of who you really are.

God loves all his children equally, and that means that he loves without judgment. We are part of God; does God judge himself? God did not give us free will only to take it away from us. That would be defeating the purpose of why we are here.

Who created judgment? We did. To judge means to take an authoritative position. *Authority* suggests persons in command or persons who govern. Perhaps we should also reevaluate our idea of government, because no being should govern anyone or anything. To *separate* means to disunite, disconnect or cease to be together. The list goes on. Why do we continue to use these negative concepts in our lives? What would happen if we used only positive ones?

Be grateful to God for our free will, because it is teaching us who we are and who we are not. We all have choices, and it is God who allows this. Without judgment in our minds and hearts, judgment would not exist.

When you understand who you are, you will realize that every day is a religious day—not only Sundays or the days set aside on religious calendars. Every day that you are here in this short incarnation is a holy day. Consider yourself lucky to be here.

There has never been such a special time in the history of our planet to be here as now. I'm sure there's a long line in the spirit world waiting to incarnate upon this planet. We are witnessing many changes and we have a great opportunity to be part of them. We can experience tremendous leaps in the evolution of our own souls as well as all others upon this small planet called Earth. The faster our souls learn to love, the faster we can all go home.

It's a sad thing to enter the spirit world and only then realize God exists. I am here to help awaken you, save you time, and maybe even save your entire lifetime.

Some souls realize they could have done better in life, but now have to wait in line to return here. Why do some people have to die to know who God is? God is all that is, and we are all connected to him. We are never separate from God or each other. We create separation to our disadvantage.

Next time you're alone, say God's name silently or aloud. Some of you will wonder why you have goosebumps. When you acknowledge God, God acknowledges you. You will sense his unconditional love for you.

God never abandons us even though some of us have abandoned him. God is always there to talk or cry to. God waits patiently to hear from us. He waits for us to open our hearts to receive him. He wants us to experience joy and laughter in our lives. It's enough to say a few words like, "How's it going, God?" It's as simple as that. We are the ones who make it complicated.

God speaks to all people who listen and hear his

messages. Love yourself as God loves you. Love others as you love yourself. Love all living creatures as God loves them. Love God every day of your life, and you will witness the creation of your Garden of Eden.

Other people can try to influence you or to place the fear in you that God doesn't exist or that he is a judging God. After reading this chapter, I hope you will know without a doubt that God is the Creator of all that exists. The forces of good and love are winning the war over fear and evil that has been taking place on this planet. Where love exists, fear is banished. When all seems to be in chaos around you, have faith in God and send blessings into the dark corners of negativity.

Read and reread this simple message and apply it in your everyday life. Remember that when you tune in to God in thought, speech or prayer, he will send you his legions of angels to guide you and illuminate your higher path. Trust in your intuition, and you will know and feel the truth. Remember that God created life itself, but what you make of it is up to you.

God is only a thought away. It's time for some of us to phone home and check in once in a while. Everyone loves to receive a phone call, even God! He also likes to call us, but often we're too busy or our answering machine is turned on. God doesn't have an answering machine, because he is always there, patiently awaiting our call.

*Love Your
Planet Earth*

Love Your Planet Earth

*L*ove your planet Earth with all your heart. This is it, folks. This is your only home at this time in your being.

Mother Earth can withstand only so much punishment from us. I think some of us have taken great advantage of her but even so, she still continues to give us a place to live. How long can we take advantage of her and not expect to be thrown out?

Mother Earth's tears flood our homes with torrential downpours. Her body rumbles with pain from the toxic environments we have created. Earthquakes and volcanic eruptions are her way of telling us that she can't ingest these poisons anymore. Hurricanes, tornadoes and severe thunderstorms are her way of unleashing her frustrations and anguish. How many more disasters do we need to get the message?

Who do we think created Mother Earth? God did. Therefore we must assume that some of us don't respect or love God. If we did, we would not allow such destructive behavior to continue.

Negative actions like destroy, ruin, crash, catastrophe, extinction, annihilation, demolish, extermination, eradication, killing off, wiping out, putting an end to, crumbling into dust, and throwing overboard can be changed and formed into a positive action. We can use creative rather than destructive ideas. Every word we use has a power of its own. Thoughts will ultimately be acted upon, and giving voice to those thoughts increases their power, accelerating their manifestation on a physical level. Have we all mastered creation on a positive physical level?

Think of the power of your negative or positive thoughts as they gather within the ethers of this planet. Like attracts like, and your thoughts manifest in matter, which creates your reality and the reality of others. What you think, speak and do creates your present and future. The more you join with others and speak about prophecies of doom, the more likely are those scenarios, just as your everyday actions and inactions further Earth's depletion. The more powerful your thoughts, the more powerful the outcome.

Dear children of planet Earth, awaken and remember who you are. The ascended masters, hierarchy, angels and beings of light from other star systems have come to assist in this cleaning-up process, but they need your help. Pass the word to others who will listen. If people ignore you, bless them and move on. Do not spend your energy or time trying to convince them about the shape the planet is in. These poor souls are not ready because they choose not to awaken and are blinded by their own fears.

Great beings of light are positioned on different parts of our planet and have been here for quite some time. They have been channeling knowledge to all those who will tune in, not just to people who are psychic or who channel. They are available to all who will listen.

Some of their messages are projected into our auric fields, then are written or spoken by us. Some of these beings of light are cleaning up our negative thought forms within the ethers and other dimensions. They also see the effects of our positive thought forms. They are helping us help ourselves, so let's keep up our positive thinking, for them as well as ourselves.

Pure unconditional love from each person can have a great impact on the future of beloved planet Earth. You are here at this time because you choose to be here. You knew when you were in spirit form that you wanted to incarnate to the Earth plane to assist in any way you could. I am here to remind you of that and wake you up. Do not take for granted the powers that God has given you. Every one of you is capable of creating or uncreating your physical environment.

We are nearing the finish line, so let's not give up now. We have come very far and are ready for change and the Garden of Eden. Sometimes we need that extra leap of faith to get over the highest obstacles. That faith is the core of where magic is born.

Learn to utilize your free will wisely, in a positive and creative way. Within the spirit world, beings of light travel and create and uncreate by means of thoughts. They visit and see anyone they wish to see. Their thoughts take them to destinations, as quickly as they think it. Dear ones of planet Earth, you too are creating and visiting with your thoughts, either consciously or unconsciously.

There are many skeptical people in the world. This might even include yourself. Do you have to see or hear a baby in a mother's womb to know it's there? Use your senses and feel it. Does a blind person have to see you to know you are standing in front or behind them? They rely on their senses to replace their eyes. Do you have to see God to know he exists? Close your eyes and feel him. Do you have to see positive or negative thought forms to know they are real? Feel the space around you, wherever you may be.

How do you feel when you enter a room filled with people? Irritable and annoyed, or happy and uplifted? Do you sometimes feel like you can't wait to leave but don't know why? This is because your higher self sensed other people's vibrations and thought forms. When you are a loving person with positive, loving people, the environment is positive and loving. When you are a negative person and are with positive people, sometimes you want to run away because you are not ready to change. When you're a loving person around negative people, you can feel the negative vibrations. You don't have to see them to know they exist. So why do some people need to see thought forms to believe they are real?

By the way, *skeptical* means doubting, disbelieving, questioning, suspicious and distrusting. We could continue through the list of these negative words and their meanings. Love is open-minded whereas fear is close-minded. Love feels and therefore knows that God exists, whereas fear can't feel it and does not believe it.

When you meet a person for the first time, do you see them as right or wrong for you? No, you feel or sense they are right or wrong for you. Perhaps it might be wise to choose words more carefully, understanding how they can limit life experiences on planet Earth.

The beings of light who are here to assist us admire us for our efforts and determination to change our present condition on this planet. When we evolve to a higher level of being, they too will evolve to a higher level. They love, support and admire us because we are the ones who chose to be in these Earth suits and within this physical arena at this time. They know it is not easy for us, and would like us to know we are not alone. Although some people can't physically see these light beings, that doesn't mean they are not here. They are here to guide us, but ultimately it is up to us to determine the final outcome.

When you help spread the word about The Ten Commitments of Love, you are already assisting, but if you want to do more, I suggest reading Dr. Joshua David Stone's series of books. His books explain in more depth about the Hierarchy council with whom you can communicate in order to pursue advanced forms of healing on planet Earth. He has written a condensed, easy-to-read encyclopedia of the spiritual path. This series explores the world's great religions, great masters, spiritual councils and the teachings of the ascended masters on spiritual growth.

There are many people who are full of greed upon this planet. Greed fills their hearts and minds. They never seem to have enough money. Insatiable greed that destroys the planet does not happen without profound spiritual consequences to those people.

The universal laws of cause and effect are in force and cannot be avoided. Haven't these people destroyed enough land and upset enough ecological systems? Have they not killed enough trees to build their developments or sold enough lumber for selfish purposes, all in the name of profit? Why haven't they heeded the warnings of Mother Earth? Will their children or children's children have a place to live in the future? These questions and many more are of no concern to these people. They are living for number one and have forgotten that we are all here together on the same planet.

We should think twice before emulating their greed and fear. We can choose not to buy their land, wood and other products. I said "their" because these people think the Earth is theirs to destroy. What they don't understand is that Mother Earth is on loan to them to live on, not to hoard her bounty or destroy her. They have forgotten the laws of cause and effect and do not believe there will be negative consequences from their actions.

Love thy planet Earth, respect her and care for her, because she is the only home we have. Remember this: Mother Earth has given us a place to live out our many lives. The people who are in the process of destroying her will have to account for their actions, but we can do our part to clean her up. The more loving thoughts we send her, the faster she can recover and become our paradise. *Paradise* suggests Eden, heaven, promised land, land of milk and honey, utopia, bliss, happiness and Shangri-La. Do you think we can have heaven on Earth? You betcha! Remember how powerful we are: We can create anything we want, including heaven on Earth!

There are no external limits to what we can create as human beings, but we limit ourselves. If we think we can't change the world, we won't. If we have faith in ourselves, others and God and believe we can change the world, we will. The choice is ours. It's about time we chose wisely, and then we will really know the meaning of *evolved beings*. Live these lessons, and we shall have our heaven on Earth.

Love Your Gift of
Life and Death

Love Your Gift of Life and Death

*L*ove your gift of life with all your heart. You were born to this Earth plane for a special purpose. Planet Earth is now experiencing an enormous cleansing period. You chose to incarnate at this time because you knew it would be a great opportunity to experience these changes firsthand, and you wanted to help assist in the human evolution. The only problem is, you have forgotten why you're here.

One of my main purposes in this book is to help awaken as many souls as possible from their deep sleep and remind them why they are here. Sounds easy, right? Wrong. When you try to wake people from a deep sleep, aren't they often cranky and don't they want to be left alone? It's not easy to walk up to people and tell them that they are here for a great purpose.

Some people are not ready to awaken. They are happy with their nine-to-five jobs; driving to work and then going home to eat, read or watch television; going to bed and then starting the whole routine over again the following day. This routine is their comfort zone, so when I tell people they have a great part in helping planet Earth, they don't want any part of it. They think it's too much responsibility and that they will have to give up too much in order to help. People don't realize that their part can be as simple as smiling at those they come in contact with or as advanced as helping clean up negative thought forms from the ethers.

The main message here is to awaken people to love themselves and others as God loves them. All souls on this planet have a purpose to fulfill—to lift our consciousness to a higher level of being. We must ascend beyond the third-dimensional level and into the realms of higher levels.

How do we do this? The answer is written clearly for us to understand. Each person has a responsibility to help themselves first, and—by doing so—this helps others and ultimately planet Earth. No one on this planet is separate, because we are all one and we are collectively creating our world. We can start by loving ourselves unconditionally. If we have already experienced loving ourselves, we will know how easy it is to love others. When we can truly live this way, we will raise our vibrations to higher levels, and by doing this, we also assist others as well as planet Earth.

As we lift our vibrations when we are around other people, without having to talk, our vibrations blend into their auric fields. We are actually creating love vibrations within the space around us, and as this vibration reaches others, they in turn will pass it to all the people with whom they come in contact. The higher the love vibration, the farther it spreads out and the more people it reaches. The more people who do this, the faster we can evolve, and eventually we can evolve as a collective consciousness. This great responsibility that we all seem to fear is simply to love self, others, all living creatures and, most of all, our divine Creator, because it is God who allows us to exist.

Begin today to pray for peace. This is not about religion. This is about helping Mother Earth. Your prayers don't have to be long in order to be effective or to reach God. "I AM" is a very powerful invocation that calls forth the creative powers of the universe. By utilizing "I AM" in your prayers, you are directly charging the frequencies and causing your words to manifest even faster. When you speak aloud, you have an opportunity to be a part of the divine unfolding of the kingdom of Heaven, God's divine plan.

There is a very powerful prayer on the last page that utilizes the words "I AM." The more people who say this short prayer, the faster the human race will transmute itself into a new race of beings who are equipped with new bodies made of light. It is only a matter of Earth time for this to take place. When you say this prayer aloud, I guarantee you will feel the power of these words.

Every single person on this planet has, at some time asked himself why he is here. Now you know. Remember, this is not about the religion you were brought up with. This is about joining together to help raise the vibrations upon this small planet.

Some people are already experiencing and seeing the higher dimensions forming right in their living rooms and outside their homes. These merging dimensions look like wavy patterns of matter. If you sit in a chair in silence and begin to look around your room, you will begin to view these patterns and feel something happening. When you go outside, if you look closely you will see black or white dots or wavy patterns in the space around you. Try keeping your eyes out of focus and view this space from different directions.

The reason some of you haven't already noticed this is because you have not tried to see it. If you don't see or feel the higher dimensions, don't worry. Perhaps you are presently experiencing the third level of reality.

You will know if you are on the third level if you don't love yourself or others or are close-minded, fearful, hateful, jealous and full of the negative emotions that prevent people from experiencing the higher realms. If you have read this far, you will know how to achieve the realms of the fourth dimension and beyond.

I will give you a hint: Love and all the positive attributes that go with love, such as compassion, giving, receiving, sharing and so on, are the keys to the higher dimensions. By the way, these same attributes are lived by advanced civilizations. Therefore, sharing knowledge with others is the wisest thing you can do because you thereby help and guide others to achieve a higher level of being.

People who don't share their knowledge with others, and who segregate themselves, are fearful that others might take their jobs or know more than they do. They are living in the third dimension of this planet. They have forgotten who they are and that we are all of one mind.

When you share with others, you assist in the evolution of planet Earth. It costs nothing. You lose nothing because you still have the same level of knowledge even after sharing it with others. The only energy it takes is your time. The more people who utilize their time wisely in order to help others, the quicker people will see miracles begin to form.

Did you ever experience a person who was slow in school and who prevented the rest of the class from moving forward? When you teach or share knowledge with such a person, often they too can understand the material and arrive at the level of the rest of the class. At that point, the class as a whole can then move forward. This same scenario occurs on planet Earth as a whole. When people help each other grow, they as a collective consciousness or planet, grows and evolves. When you truly understand this, you will begin to witness these higher dimensions and know without a doubt that you are vibrating at a higher level of being.

Evolvement means unfolding, growing, expanding, changing, improving, mutating and elaborating. When you experience the higher realms, you will know that your present reality is only an illusion for the purpose of your soul's evolvement. Your illusion can be changed at any time. Your illusion can be changed by simply shifting your consciousness, which means thinking, speaking and performing acts of love for self and others. When you love yourself and others, you allow yourself to move into higher dimensions, because higher realms only function with love.

How many more books have to be written for us to remember who we are? How much more time will we waste before we begin to love each other? Every book takes years to unfold, to become published, to reach the bookstores, and only then can it fall into our hands. After the book is purchased, it is either read or placed under a stack of other unread books. Finally, after reading the books, we are impressed with certain inspirational words of wisdom to use for our next step. Do we think that perhaps somebody has been trying to tell us something?

Does God need to stand on a mountaintop to shout his simple message of love? No, God is busy creating and therefore sends messengers, his angels and guides, to deliver the messages. Does the postmaster deliver mail to people? No, he or she sends mail carriers to deliver the mail. God has given us the gift of life; it is up to us what we do with our life and the messages we receive. God sends the message, which is delivered directly to us. We then choose whether or not we want to receive it.

People who write books or music are channeling the words from their higher selves through the higher dimensions of consciousness. Books, though written by an author, are often really channeled from spirit guides, archangels, ascended masters and beings of light from other star systems. Some book covers print the name of the author as well as the guide or light being the author channeled. Some of these books can be found at your local New Age bookstores. All these books, including this one, contain similar messages about love—messages that are sent by God and channeled from spirits. The messages were gathered and written by the author, then passed on to the people of planet Earth.

The Brotherhood of Light, which is called the Great White Brotherhood, wants us to move into the next century as a higher level of beings. We have come a long way but still have work to do. The spirit world is assisting as much as they can by guiding us, but they cannot interfere with our free will. It is up to us to create what we want and decide in which dimension we want to reside.

I still have some bugs to work out, but I'm learning just like you are. I don't like to sit and wait for things to be handed to me. I prefer to jump in and actively pursue life. When you know you have given it your best shot, there is nothing like the feeling of celebration afterwards. People who have moved mountains in their lives often had to get out and push. Are you giving your present lifetime your best shot, or are you sitting at the sidelines waiting for your life to take off?

I personally think that some of us can do better, but we are afraid of failure or of standing in the limelight. Some people are fearful of success because in order to succeed they will have to move out of their comfort zone. We have plenty of time to rest after death, but unless we walk out of our comfort zones now, how will we know if we are fully alive or not? To truly live is to experience life to its fullest potential and to go into the world and make a difference.

We can fail only if we think of ourselves as failures. Failure is considered a learning experience, a means to learn to do better. Perhaps we can change the meaning of *failure* to "a prelude to success" because through failure we learn to do better. It's a term we can redefine and feel differently about, letting our setbacks assist us on our paths.

People use the word *failure* a lot, but maybe now is the time to begin deleting it from our minds' computer. We have to reprogram our thinking to contain positive concepts and words that lift the spirit.

Being out in the limelight can be a bit scary, but isn't it a glorious place to be? We are able to share with others our words of wisdom and reach people on a larger scale. Think of all the lives we can touch by getting out of our comfort zone. The potential is unlimited and so is our evolvement.

Help spread the word, because word of mouth and personal experience is the fastest way for spiritual ideas to travel. Do you recall telling someone in the office about something, and by the time you walked to the other end of the building, your words had already arrived there?

Let's not waste time, because we are only here for an instant to accomplish our tasks. How many more years can Mother Earth withstand our foolish behaviors? This statement is not directed at anyone in particular. Those who are responsible know who they are.

Let's not wait until we are dead to realize we could have done better. When I make my transition into the spirit world, I'm making sure that I'll be celebrating with my guides, angels, loved ones and whoever else has on a party hat. I don't want to carry any regrets about how I could have done better or reached more people or that I was too stagnant.

By each one shifting his consciousness, life will become easier for everyone, because more higher vibrations will emanate throughout the planet. Think of yourself as a light warrior who is clearing a path for others to follow. It is no mistake that you are reading this book, because you were guided to do so by your higher self and spirit guides.

Some of you have been feeling uneasy, irritable and unwell but don't know why. Some of these physical and emotional changes are caused by the shift that has already begun with the merging of the higher dimensions. The shift is explained in more detail in Dr. Joshua David Stone's series and *The Keys of Enoch* by J.J. Hurtak.

This shift is actually changing the DNA within our bodies. If my guides felt this knowledge was not to be known, I would not have written these words. The hierarchy council must feel that we are ready for truth and an explanation about what is taking place on this planet and in our entire universe. Our bodies are trying to adjust to the higher frequencies and our physical structures are accommodating more light. This process is preparing us to become a new race of beings and ascend into lightbody vehicles. This knowledge is difficult for some people to accept, but nevertheless, this is what is now taking place.

People who choose love for their reality are experiencing minor discomforts. People who choose fear, anger and hatred are having an even more difficult time adjusting to these higher frequencies. As a matter of fact, the more they fear, the more they intensify these unpleasant discomforts, causing more chaos in their lives and the lives of others. The more you give in to these fears, the stronger their grip and the more discomfort you will experience. These fears are the hatred and rage that people feel for themselves as well as others. When you reduce the fears, you lessen their grip, until love finally releases you and sets you free.

By reading this chapter, you will realize that you are at the right place and the right time. There are souls waiting to be born to experience this great event. Be grateful that you are here for the opportunity to witness firsthand the evolution of the human race. Don't take your life for granted, because there are many souls who would love to be in your place. Don't waste a single instant in your life.

The spirit world is rooting for us and standing by our sides because we are all on the same team. We should never feel that we are better or worse than other people, because we are all equal and trying to accomplish the same job.

If it weren't for the factory workers who produce the products, the executive officers and owners would not have jobs and the companies would be out of business. If it weren't for the marketing people who sell the products, the factory workers wouldn't have jobs. This goes on and on, ultimately resting in the hands of the consumers. So you see, no one is higher or lower than another. All people are team members and combine their talents to get any job done. We as a human race are all on the same team and are combining our individual talents to transcend to a higher level of consciousness. The only reason there are separate countries around the world is because we drew lines on a map and on the Earth to make them separate. In reality, a line can be erased at any given time.

I once had a job in management and was told not
to associate with the factory workers. I realized that I
enjoyed communicating with them because some of
them were down-to-earth people, while those in
management appeared to be stuffy and always
seemed to worry what others were wearing that day.
The managers seldom laughed, and some thought
they were more important than the factory workers
because they wore nicer clothes, had better work-
spaces and made more money.

One day I realized that I'd decide for myself with
whom I would associate. After that I started meeting
with the factory workers on my breaks and lunches,
which led to the other managers shunning me and
trying in every way possible to make me feel uncomfortable. I eventually allowed myself to feel bad and
began doubting myself and what I was doing.

One day one of the factory workers said,
"Michele, I just wanted to thank you for being kind
to me because you make me feel like a real person. I
consider you my friend." After I heard this, I realized
that I was upset only because I was out of my comfort zone, and that nobody else had the guts to stand
up for what they believed in or for their preferences
in associates. They feared getting fired, being
harassed or feeling out of place. These are common
experiences of being out of your comfort zone, but
the rewards for sticking it out are well worth it. Some
people might shun you but eventually they let you
be yourself. All it takes is one person to stand up for

what he or she believes in. Others will eventually
follow.

I will never forget that factory worker's comment,
which was reiterated by the other workers. The comment would not have been made if I hadn't stepped
away from my comfort zone. At that time, the only
difference between the other management people's
approach versus my own, was that I didn't view
myself as separate from others.

You must learn to believe in yourself and have
faith that God will guide you. What do you think
would have happened if Martin Luther King or
Gandhi had decided to stay within his comfort zone?
No speeches would have been written, no voices
would have been heard and people would not have
been shown a higher path to follow. Both King and
Gandhi talked about equality for all people. They not
only each had a dream, but they also helped us realize that dream in our lives. Today, everyone needs to
continue this dream and make it a reality. This is
how advanced civilizations operate and exist—by
ensuring equality for all beings and by living the
principles of love and compassion. Without these
virtues, civilizations gradually cease to exist.

When we allow our hearts to be filled with love,
we can travel the ethers and create our new world.
There are no limits to how much love we can spread.
If we are filled with love, we can never burn out or
become empty. God's continuous love energy enters
at the top of our heads, or crown chakras. We in turn

decide by our free will either to pass this love to others or not.

Appreciate the gift of life that God has given you and be grateful for each day you are here because you never know when it will be your last. There has never been a more interesting time in history to be on this planet than now. Remember that you are not alone. Your loved ones in spirit are rooting for you all the way. Soon everyone can join together and celebrate the birth of a New World. Everyone will be dancing, everyone will be laughing, you can be sure.

Also love your gift of death. Do not be afraid of dying. The process of death is a going home. Death is a portal to the spirit world, and you are simply releasing the physical body to go on in your spirit body. Remember that your physical body is for learning and experiencing your lessons for the purpose of evolving. Your real vehicle is not the physical body but your spirit body. Death is like taking off your heavy clothes after work. It's a great release to shed your physical body at death, for you are free from the heaviness of the old clothes.

When souls suffer from pain and disease, death is often a great release, because after death these souls will no longer have the pain or burden of their physical vehicle. To occupy a physical body only means that you need such a vehicle in order to experience the dense matter of this planet. Death is a resting period or pit stop for all the trials and tribulations you've experienced while in the physical body. It is a time of rest, when each person gets spiritually recharged. You had a choice to incarnate on this planet. Other souls chose to learn their lessons on other planets and universes. Earth is one of the most difficult schools—you knew that when you chose it.

Some people think of death as an ending when their physical existence ceases, after which they will no longer see their loved ones. This is far from the truth. There is clear evidence today that life after death exists. Such evidence is overwhelming. Some people will be in for a surprise when they awaken in the spirit world and see Uncle Henry. Death is a new beginning as well as a transition to other planes of existence. A person's death might be viewed as the start of new adventure, because one gets to choose where one is going to go next.

Actually, at birth it's more difficult to enter a mother's womb as an unborn child than it is to enter the spirit world when we die. This is because when we die, we take our personalities with us, but at birth we have to adjust to the new difficulty in communicating with one's family, as well as to the confinement of the physical body.

As we grow as children, we slowly forget our former existences, why we chose to come here and what life's lessons we came here to learn. Sometimes we see a baby or a small child talk or laugh at something that is not there. We adults may have seen nothing, but the child was probably seeing a loved one, a guide or an angel from the spirit realm.

When you're in the spirit world, you create things by thought. You can visit loved ones in the spirit realm as well as on the Earth plane. The veils are gone and you are exposed to memories of your past lives as well as lessons you set out to experience while on the Earth plane.

When you enter the spirit world, you bring with you your personality and your sense of humor, but not your physical vehicle. Did you ever hear a psychic or channeler say that Uncle Joe still has his sense of humor and wears the same brown hat?

There are many people today who perform readings. Some of these people are genuine while others are not. The ones who are not will have to account for their untruthful words and the ripple effect caused by their actions. The ones who are real have given information to grieving families that they could not possibly have known without access to the spirit world.

For example, some psychics mention nicknames of the deceased, his favorite shirt, what Aunt Mary got her for Christmas, a favorite movie or saying, the cause or place of death—the list goes on. These true readers or psychics ask only for your first name when you go for a reading.

A particularly intuitive reader is George Anderson. George has written many books, performs lectures, appears on talk and radio shows and gives individual and group readings. His present waiting list is about a year or more. This man has helped many people over the years and has proven without a doubt that there is life after death. I suggest reading his books and deciding for yourself. There are many more like him. Some are currently working with the FBI and police departments to solve violent crimes. Do you think the FBI or the police would waste their time if these people weren't effective? Some of these psychics have already solved some of the most baffling and horrendous crimes.

There is more than enough evidence today to substantiate the truth of life after death. Were you ever in a room and felt a presence or had chills run up your spine? Perhaps a loved one stopped in to say hello or was simply trying to get your attention. They hear you from your vibrations, which are heard in all dimensions of reality. They see all your trials and tribulations. At times they join in to celebrate birthdays, graduations, holidays or other special events. Sometimes a grandparent from the spirit world may even sit beside you and watch a grandchild play a baseball game or dance in a ballet recital. Do you need to see a loved one to know he or she is there? Learn to use your intuition and feelings, and you will be surprised at how much you will experience. The more you open up, the more the spirit realm opens up to you.

To accommodate us, loved ones are willing to expend the great amount of energy necessary to materialize themselves. Because of this, we might think twice before asking them for help. Spirits know that human beings are easily startled, which is why some spirits prefer to be seen in our peripheral vision. Our guides and loved ones from the spirit realm understand our limitations and know how much we can handle at any particular time.

In conclusion, my advice is to love your gifts of life and death, because they have led you to whom you are today and will lead you to whom you will become tomorrow. Birth is an entering into Earth life, whereas death is an entering into spirit life; both are glorious moments of existence.

VII

Love Your
Work

Love Your Work

*L*ove your work with all your heart and soul. You have a choice of what work you want to do while you are here on Earth. God does not intend for us to be miserable with our jobs. If you are unhappy with your job, change it; do something else. Who said you cannot change a job at will? I'm sad to see so many people unhappy and dissatisfied with their work. God has given mankind free will and it is people's own choices that make them happy or sad.

Many unhappy people stay with their jobs for too many years. Why? Because they fear change, fear losing so many years' investment, fear starting over, fear losing benefits and accumulated vacation time, fear missing their friends and co-workers, fear losing time looking for another job, fear losing a needed level of pay, fear having too many skills or not enough for a new job and so on. All their excuses are fear-oriented.

Some people complain daily about their jobs and swear they're going to quit but still remain in their positions for years. They complain about bosses, co-workers, unfair wages and unhealthy or unfair working conditions.

Each day such people become more and more unhappy and lay their frustrations upon family and friends. This in turn makes family and friends uneasy and unsure of how to respond. They most likely will say, "Get another job." That is not what unhappy people want to hear. The advice often triggers an irritable response toward the new antagonist. Unhappy people take out their frustrations on anyone who crosses their paths and thus begins a ripple effect.

Unhappiness permeates all other areas of these people's lives. Their unhappiness with their work begins to affect health and relationships. Nothing seems to go right no matter what they do. Their health declines because they have manifested the disease of fear into their physical bodies. All the anger, frustration and sadness, after playing havoc with mind and emotions, eventually take their toll on physical health.

At this point people begin to seek the help of doctors, therapists, psychics, the family priest and even God himself to find answers to their problems. Family and friends grow tired of hearing them complain, especially when they don't take steps to solve their problems.

No one knows what to do for these poor souls. They feel lost and think no one can understand how they feel or what they are experiencing. When this happens, it puts a tremendous strain on relationships. When someone is so unhappy with his or her work, it inevitably affects family and friends, eventually leading to arguments, hurt feelings, resentments, gloom and damaged relationships.

Such people lose their desire to entertain at home or attend social functions. They often prefer to watch television or hang out at the local bar in order to complain some more. They stop doing what they once enjoyed; they yell at the dog or cat. Children get on their nerves because they lose their patience so easily.

Their personalities change, and their loved ones insist that they do not know them anymore. This has a negative effect on their sex lives. Those who are drowning in unhappiness have no energy left for lovemaking, or feel they cannot please their partners as they once did. The loved ones feel uneasy because they don't recognize the persons they once loved. Many times this leads to difficult breakups or dissatisfied relationships.

Some people who hate their work take their hatred out of the workplace with them. Everything becomes an excuse to express bottled-up anger. Driving on the streets today can be very dangerous because too many people are consumed by frustration.

Some people play ego games on the road with

their lives and the lives of others. They think they're invincible as they weave between other vehicles. Some even stop using blinkers because they either forget or are not concerned with other drivers. They give people obscene gestures while they run other drivers off the road.

These foolish behaviors have led to unnecessary accidents, shootings and tragic deaths. Many lives would be spared if only these people could love instead of fear. Taking your frustrations out on the road is dangerous both to yourself and those who are simply trying to get to their destinations. When you love others, you are a caring, courteous driver at all times and value your life as well as the lives of others.

This chapter will probably hit home for many people. Our work is a big part of our lives because we spend so much of our time there. People who are unhappy with their work are wasting much precious time. Some of us have had parents who were miserable in their jobs until they finally retired. Some people never make it to retirement because they die prematurely from stress. Consequently, they don't get to spend their hard-earned money. In their retirement years they never reap the expected reward for their past suffering.

Those who do make it to retirement, often get heart disease, cancer or arthritis. In bitterness, they realize that they've wasted their lives in unfulfilling jobs. Why do they realize this in retirement? Because in retirement they have time to ponder over their earlier lives.

This is a very sad experience for humans. Some wish they could start over and get second chances. Others insist things would have been different if only they had followed their dreams and not the dreams of others. When you reach retirement age, you start to assess your life and wonder if you could have done better. You might have obtained certain benefits for sticking it out all those years but those benefits may not be worth the pain you endured. Do you think then, they should be called benefits? Is there a less painful way of creating our own benefits?

A friend informed me that she had invested thirty years of her life with a company she has been dissatisfied with. Despite her dissatisfaction, she had saved enough money to retire early. The company for which she had made so much money told her that she would be penalized by 40 per cent for her decision to retire early. My friend felt she could not afford to lose that amount of money, so she decided to stay the remaining years and help make more money for this company. Do you think she is now angry, disappointed, sad, hurt and bitter? Do you think that by the time she can retire, she will be able to climb mountains or play hours of tennis each day as easily as before?

In spite of how painful this was for her, she decided to stay. Even though she had been a good worker for many years, her company could still decide to decrease her benefits. This was a very painful lesson. It seldom pays to remain at a job you are unhappy with. Your personal cost is incalculable, and the rewards you expect may not be forthcoming in the end.

What's surprising is that this particular company is a large one and could have easily filled the position. This tragic situation happens to many people on this planet. Companies are so greedy that they penalize their own family, so to speak. People who greedily accumulate money, shortchanging the workers who make it possible, are at the mercy of the law of cause and effect.

Who invented retirement? I think individuals should decide at what age they would like to retire, and they should be able to do so without being penalized. Why do we have to wait until we're too old or ill to enjoy our remaining years? This retirement age guideline will change when we as a people decide it no longer serves us. We created it and we have the power to uncreate it or change it to fit our current needs.

The love of money is the root of all evil, but we all need money to survive. We all count on health-care benefits. We need money for roofs over our heads, for food, for education, for running and maintaining our vehicles and homes, for paying bills and (if there's anything left over) for entertainment or vacations. No wonder why people feel pressured to remain at well-paying jobs.

To add to the stress, we also need money to cover our funeral expenses so that our loved ones won't be stuck with the bills. We even need money to pay for childbirth. The minute we come out of our mother's womb the tab starts, although before birth, our parents paid the bills. If some of us had known in advance about the money involved, we might have returned to the spirit world while we had the chance.

No wonder the credit card business is booming! People don't have enough money for the quality of life they want, so they charge it. Then they pay penalties or finance charges on top of the money they borrowed. Some people even use credit cards to buy food. Bankruptcies are soaring because people fall further and further behind economically. Once they declare bankruptcy, they have no credit and then must rely on their incomes to buy everything. The reason they used their credit cards in the first place was because the cost of what they considered necessities exceeded their incomes.

At this point, such people usually hunt down second or third jobs on top of the stressful ones they already have. They start borrowing money from family members and friends but cannot pay them back for years, if at all. If they miss a day of work from illness, they fall even further behind. It's understandable why people can't afford to be sick, especially when they have no health benefits or sick time.

Some people in this situation contemplate robberies. Isn't there something wrong with our system

and this picture? It's about time we talk to our so-
called leaders and turn this picture around. It is up to
all of us to decide what we want to create.

Here are a few things I, as a leader, would begin
to implement on my first day in office: All monies
would immediately be redistributed for the good of
all people. All weapons of destruction would be dis-
mantled and destroyed.

Most people do not know the following information, because it was kept secret from the people of
planet Earth. Back in the 1950s very advanced
extraterrestrials offered to help with Earth people's
technological, medical and spiritual problems. They
stipulated only one requirement in exchange for their
help, which was that all nuclear weapons be disman-
tled and destroyed. The government refused. If you
would like to know more about the secret government, I strongly suggest reading Dr. Joshua David
Stone's *Hidden Mysteries*. I was very surprised by the
information in it. I guarantee that you won't be disappointed.

It's time for people to wake up and know the
truth, because it has been hidden for many years.
Fear keeps the truth from us. Love opens the door
and sets it free. What we do with it is up to all of us.

It's important that not a single dangerous and
unhealthy food will be allowed to enter our food
markets. All production of petrochemicals will cease
and all stored chemicals will be destroyed. Organic
foods will provide sustenance for every person on

planet Earth. Not a single person or child will ever go without food or drink again. Every single mind-altering product will be destroyed, including street drugs, alcoholic beverages and tobacco. Never again will these harmful substances be placed in the hands of our children and jeopardize the future of all children on planet Earth.

Only natural energy will be used to run our vehicles, homes and workplaces. There will be no need for electric wires, poles, cables or powerhouses. Instead, we will use the greatest technology known to man—crystals.

Ancient people utilized these precious minerals. They knew about their great powers and the unending possibilities of the technology. We choose not to make use because of the investment in our present systems. Greed and fear of change are the culprits again, and so is our secret government. What would happen if we no longer needed oil and gasoline? Do we need to have wars to switch over to these new sources of energy? There are many more things I would do if I were leader of the planet, but it would take a whole book to mention them all.

Do you think I'm just dreaming about the better world I've described? Didn't our elders say that if we wished hard enough, our dreams could come true and become a reality? By recording my dreams of a better world, I help bring the dream into reality. Never underestimate your dreams because visions are the precursors of the world's greatest inventions.

They may someday be brought into our physical environment on Earth.

Perhaps if we did away with the dollar, we would witness a massive, positive change in our society. We would learn to help others and ourselves by trading our services. I think people in the old days saw that such a system had many benefits. When you exchange with others, you are sharing, and both parties benefit.

The greatest of all job satisfactions is the service of our fellow human beings. There is no greater joy and happiness than assisting others accomplish their dreams. By helping them, we in turn are fulfilled. Give to others and we will receive tenfold back. When both giving and sharing is done from the heart, no amount of money can equal the personal satisfaction we receive.

The love of money is the root of all evil because it separates humans from each other. If we sit and ponder over the way money and the greed that surrounds it harms others, we will see the benefit of freeing ourselves. Some people fear never having enough or always having too little. I think it's time we began to speak up, get out of our comfort zones and not waste any more of our precious years following the crowd. We need to understand why our society is in its present condition.

We humans need to accelerate to the fast track so that we can catch up to the other advanced civilizations. I call them advanced and civilized beings because they live in the higher vibrations of love and they create and utilize the powers that God has given all. They realize that life and civilization are synonymous.

These intelligent beings are considered advanced because they know that anything less than love eventually leads to the annihilation of the group consciousness. The history of planetary civilizations shows this sort of period as now. Whether a civilization annihilates itself or corrects its imbalances, it is an inevitable stage of every civilization.

Some of our technologies are good ones, but if we are not advanced spiritually, we can't evolve or advance to higher levels of consciousness. It's important to share knowledge with others so that we can evolve as a whole, which will in turn advance our planet.

Love your work with all your heart, because you are here for a short time, and that time is too precious to waste. Sit alone in silence and think about your work. You will know if you are happy or not. If you are unhappy, you have a choice to stay, to leave or to change the situation. The decision is yours. No decision is right or wrong. You are choosing between creating for your reality a satisfying and fulfilling job that can help others or a dissatisfying and unfulfilling job that helps no one.

If you decide to stay where you are unhappy, you only have yourself to blame. You cannot blame your boss, co-workers, the pay, the benefits, the work itself, your family, friends or God. If you cannot break away, perhaps you can make the best of it by simply shifting your conscious thoughts to positive ones. By doing this, you can create a more comfortable environment.

Equipped with knowledge from chapters one and two, you know that each soul is evolving at its own pace. Maybe one of your lessons is patience, understanding, compassion or the courage to move forward toward a better opportunity. When you recognize and acknowledge change in your life and wonder why things or feelings change, especially when you felt you were comfortable with your life, realize that there is always a good reason. There is a new opportunity for a learning experience and soul growth. Be aware of your evolvement as a soul. Perhaps after being at a job for many years, your soul becomes bored and wants to expand its experience or find other ways to help others.

One of the most rewarding jobs on this planet is service to others. When you help others in unselfish ways, you in turn will receive. The more people you help, the more they will help others. This creates a ripple effect. Acts of kindness can help lift the vibration on this planet more than you know.

Remember that when you love yourself and others, opportunities will come your way. They can manifest in many forms, such as bumping into a stranger when you're out walking or speaking to an old friend you haven't seen in a while. Such an exchange can bring about an opportunity that leads to the challenging job you've been searching for. Your conversation might be simply about ideas for a career change, or you might learn of a company that has been looking for help in your field. When you're kind to the universe, the universe is kind to you.

Always have an open mind because you never know what opportunities may come into your life or how many people you can help as a result of an unexpected opportunity. One way your guides assist you is through other people. Your spirit guides can direct you to a new book, a magazine article, a song on the radio, a new or old movie or a new job where you can be of greater service.

When you love yourself and others, your vibration changes, and you will be surprised at all the good you attract. If you somehow attract a not-so-nice person, there is a purpose to that, too. Either they needed to learn something from you or you needed to learn from them (it usually is both). There are no coincidences. Everything happens according to God's divine plan and at exactly the right time.

Perhaps you need to learn something at your present job before your soul feels it's the right time to move forward. Put your ego aside and assess yourself. Do you need to work on negative behaviors at this moment in your being? By assessing yourself, you will most likely find the answers you have been seeking. The answers have, and will always be, within you.

Remember that you are creating your reality for your soul's evolvement. If you are not happy, there is something you need to work out with yourself. Others can give you advice, but you have to make the final decision. Learn to be your own adviser. It costs nothing, and you become familiar with your own strengths and the areas that still need work.

Let's not have any regrets when we reach our retirement years. Our souls always knew planet Earth was the best school in the universe. We should consider ourselves lucky to have been accepted. It is never too late to attain knowledge for the growth of our souls, nor is it too late to learn new skills or trades. We are the ones who place limits on ourselves. Let's soar above and beyond what we think we're capable of. Do not be afraid of change, because change will help us become the advanced beings we're meant to be. There are no limits to how many people we can reach or how much we can change another person's life for the better.

VIII

Love Your Place of Residence

Love Your Place
of Residence

*L*ove your place of residence and be thankful to God that you have a roof over your head. Some people on planet Earth are homeless. There might be a reason for being where you currently are. Have you asked yourself if there is anyone living around you whom you can help in any way? Can you make someone's life brighter by being there for them? Remember that when you help others, if you do it from the heart, you do not expect anything in return.

We must not turn down anyone who truly needs our help. God sometimes tests us to see if we're sincere or not. He even tests us when we've had a hard day to see if we remember who we really are. Helping others is not only for certain days. Helping others should be a continuous act of love.

There are no set guidelines about when God

wants to wake us up. Remember that we are all on this planet together, experiencing similar trials and tribulations. Our hearts may appear small in size, but they have the capacity to reach out to every human being on this planet.

Appreciate and be grateful for all that you have because it is probably far more than people have in other countries. *Gratitude* means gratefulness, thankfulness, acknowledgment, recognition and thanksgiving for one's gifts in life and blessing one's lucky stars. When you are grateful for what you have, including the roof over your head, you set in motion universal laws that assist you in receiving those very gifts.

We are all God's children and are worthy to receive his great abundance. When we share our abundance, we increase it. We are not meant to hoard our abundance, for it is on loan to us and to be shared with others. All things belong to God. They are for our use and enjoyment while we are in our physical bodies.

Share this knowledge with others and tell them to pass the gift of giving to someone else. The moment you give to another, you are immediately repaid. Do you remember the happy feeling you had when you gave a gift to someone? That unselfish act caused a ripple effect so that your positive energy is now spreading out to others. You will review these positive effects upon your death at your life review. Also, somewhere, sometime you will be given a gift, not necessarily a material gift, but a gift of love.

You may witness people on this planet hoarding their abundance, but be assured that upon their deaths they will have to assess their lives. Sometimes double assessments take place, from the Earth courtroom as well as the spirit world. When you are greedy in this lifetime, you will have to repay it in some way, either in this life or in your next lifetime. Some people think they are cheating others, but in reality they are only cheating themselves.

There is no escaping when one has broken God's laws. There is no punishment, but there is a delay in the evolvement of one's soul, which is a step backward.

Were you ever held back a grade and unable to graduate with the rest of your class? Some of you remember how you felt about repeating a whole year. Your friends were in the grade above you and were moving forward. You felt alone and had to make new friends, which wasn't easy. You had to learn the same lessons over again and try to pass this time. Also, you often forgot what the previous year's textbooks contained and could not recall the old lessons.

Think about this for a moment. Now visualize going backward on a much grander scale, such as a whole lifetime. Do you understand how devastating this can be to souls when they assess their lives after entering the spirit world? They realize that by not learning lessons from past lifetimes, they will have to repeat them next time as well as learn new ones. When a soul enters a new lifetime, it has no memory of past lessons or the lessons chosen for its new lifetime. These souls are faced with learning the lessons of their new, much more challenging lifetimes while having to catch up with older lessons in order to evolve and move forward with the rest of their soul group.

When you intentionally cause a negative situation or hurt another being, you have a direct effect on him and his life. This is called the universal law of cause and effect and is carried out by the universe. When an individual is responsible for causing harm or hurt to a large number of people, the payback will be heavy baggage.

Perhaps, after the previous paragraphs, all of us will think twice before intentionally hurting others or withholding our abundance. Isn't it easier to share and have compassion for fellow beings? My life's lessons have been difficult enough and I'd rather not repeat them. I wish to learn a whole new array of lessons in my next lifetime. I'm sure most of us would like to evolve, and we can by simply understanding the concepts of books like this and putting them into action.

God did not say to give all your abundance away, but it would be nice to surprise a friend, neighbor or stranger with a tray of baked cookies or a material object that has been sitting in your attic for years. This object may be of no use to you, but it may have meaning for someone else. At this very moment you can assess yourself to see if you're overly attached to your material possessions or not.

People who are homeless are here to teach us something. We can also teach them something. When we see a homeless person, they remind us to be grateful for what we have. Souls that have chosen to be homeless might, in a previous lifetime, have hoarded their abundance. In this lifetime they need to learn what it is like to lack abundance. This could be a lesson for them to master. Also, when they place their alms cups in front of us, maybe God is testing us to see if we are hoarding our abundance.

We can teach the homeless something by being caring, loving, compassionate people. By showing them that there are people who care about them, we might give them the impetus to get back on their feet. How many lives can we touch by simply loving others?

Each soul has a choice about whether or not he wants a roof over his head. God did not say a roof has to be built from shingles, cardboard or the night sky. Some of us judge these souls by their appearance, but we should not judge a book by its cover nor condemn the book's interior knowledge.

Each soul's book is unique in itself because it contains the true spiritual words of one's higher self. Some of us continue to view people from the outside even though the true person is within and beyond the material matter. A book or person's spirit resides inside, and not on the book cover or the body vehicle.

Did you ever reject a book because of a ripped cover with a short uninviting title printed on it? Then later when you read the book, did you realize that there was more to it than you thought? A book cover gives you a condensed idea of what's inside. Only later after you open the book do you discover a whole new world of endless plots, scenes, pictures and words.

Some homeless people are old souls incarnated here to teach us a valuable lesson. The lesson is hidden and can't be learned from their appearance. When all of us have truly learned the lesson of sharing, maybe their work will be done.

Love your place of residence because you learn something from where you live. When you feel eager to move, maybe your soul has accomplished all that it can where you are. Then it must search for a different area to reside where it can be of help to others. Next time you feel a desire to move but don't know why, it is most likely your higher self pushing you forward.

You can love your residence but do not be attached to it. It is only a material dwelling where your soul resides and experiences life. Sometimes, you have to learn very painful lessons to see whether or not you are overly attached to your home or your material wealth. Your residence and material possessions can be taken from you at any moment because of a divorce, a fire, a tornado, a flood, an earthquake, a volcano, an avalanche or even an unexpected thief.

Don't worry about thefts or loss too much. You will always remember your loved ones. Your memories of them are stored deep within your subconscious mind. You do not need pictures or material objects in order to remember the times you had with them. A soul which has no attachments to material things has evolved to a higher level of being. It's okay to acquire abundance but do not attach yourself to that abundance. Know that things are there for your use and enjoyment and if they are taken away, you will acquire different possessions for your use and enjoyment.

One of my purposes at my place of residence is to help lost souls or spirits go into the light. One day, I communicated with a spirit called John. I realized that he was attached to my house because he had died in it. He was also attached to the surrounding fields and farmland. John was still living on the Earth plane because he had been too attached to his material reality. This kind of attachment stops the soul from growing. John's loved ones were waiting for him in the light, but some souls like John cannot seem to find the light because there's so much dense matter that surrounds our planet.

When you look beyond the darkness and fear, a light seems to appear before your eyes. As you move forward toward the light, it becomes brighter and brighter until it encompasses your entire being. When souls are led into the light, they are able to see loved ones and guides in the spirit world and they can attend school there in order to advance or evolve their souls.

When I first communicated with John, he was not ready to leave the house or go into the light. We must respect a soul's free will and not place any judgments even though we might think we know what the soul's higher choice is. John had concerns about his farmland and the house he thought he still lived in. He had concerns about the changes taking place around the area and about the farmland possibly being sold to greedy developers.

I assured him that his house would be taken care of while I lived here. I also told him that it was only a material dwelling and served his soul only while he was on the material plane. I also told him that his loved ones were waiting for him in the light and that once he moved into the light himself, he would be able to visit anyone from the spirit world as well as any people on the Earth plane anytime he wanted. John, however, was still not ready to leave. Because of the free choice God has given all of us, we cannot force a soul to go into the light unless its ready and chooses to do so.

A year later as he watched me grow in my spiritual work, John finally became ready. During that year, he met my spirit guides, masters and loved ones from the spirit world. They communicated with him every now and then. John learned many things about spiritual growth and realized how important it is for us to develop spiritually while we are here on the Earth plane. Also, he learned how important it is not to overly attach ourselves to our material reality because it is only an illusion, which is created by us for the purpose of our souls' development.

John had died in the early 1960s. He was not accustomed to all the changes that occurred in the material world any more than he felt comfortable with what spirituality really was. I might say that my guides and I taught him within the Earth plane.

Hierarchy guides, masters and angels have mastered both life on the physical level and higher levels of consciousness. Some of these Hierarchy beings reside within the councils and committees of the office of the Christ. A few of the beings I communicate with and work with include the angelic Hierarchy of Michael and Raphael, as well as Abraham, Isis, Thoth and Sri Sathya Sai Baba, who is one of the greatest beings incarnated now here to help assist us in raising our consciousness.

I also communicate with a group consciousness of light beings from another star system. These light beings are here to help guide me in my healing work. They speak a universal language and are as honored to work with me as I am with them. They work with a client's auric field right down to the cellular level. As I've mentioned, disease first manifests in the emotional and mental body. These light beings help me work on all levels of the human body. They also assist me with Reiki and Seichem energies and add their own light energy to the mix.

We are all worthy enough to channel these great beings of light. We ourselves place limits on ourselves. Some of us listen to others who tell us we're not capable of communicating with such advanced beings of light. This is far from the truth. These beings are here to help lift the consciousness of planet Earth. If we are willing to call upon them, they are willing to teach and guide us.

When John was ready to go into the light, my guide, Master Thomas, and I took John's hands. John was a bit frightened, but Thomas reassured him that all would be well. Thomas illuminated the path to the tunnel, which is the portal for going into the light. When John was ready, Master Thomas let go of his hand. Thomas continued to watch John ascend through the entrance of the tunnel and into the light.

John arrived in the spirit world within Earth seconds and his loved ones and guides were there to greet him. The angels were singing and there was a great celebration because another soul had found the light. Tears of joy filled my eyes. John was at peace and no longer a lost soul. He had finally found one of God's many mansions.

The next day at about four o'clock in the morning, I felt a presence by the foot of my bed. I realized it was John visiting me to thank me for helping him and to tell me he was happy. I knew at that moment why I was meant to reside at my old house.

Work does not end within the material world. There are lost spirits or souls within the Earth plane who need to be sent to the light. I hope this chapter has opened a new door for you. There is so much work to be done that perhaps some of you will also assist in helping a lost soul find the light. I have found no greater joy than helping others on Earth as well as in spirit. Remember that there is a reason why you are at your place of residence at this time.

After John had ascended to the light, I am happy to say I sent four other spirits into the light as well. One particular spirit was an eight-year-old girl named Sara. Sara visits me quite often. She is happy now, is attending school and is with loved ones and guides once again.

If you come across spirits on your path, do not be afraid because most likely they want to be sent into the light. Your light attracts them and the more you assist in this type of work, the more you become a beacon of light for lost souls everywhere you go.

If you ever feel a little heavy or irritable, most likely a soul is eager to be sent into the light and is trying to get your attention. At that time, tell it men-tally or aloud (depending where you are) that it needs to go into the light so that it can attend school and evolve. Also, tell it its loved ones are waiting for it and that it will be able to visit the Earth plane if it chooses to do so later. Don't worry if you cannot hear the soul. It can hear you loud and clear.

If you want, you can visualize the angels with a golden net as they take the lost souls into the light. At that moment, you might feel a release or an increase in energy and feel suddenly much happier.

Some people cannot explain why they feel slug-gish or uneasy when they enter a building. Now you know that the building probably needs to be cleared. The poor souls in the building have been trying to get some attention for years but no one was con-sciously aware of them. It only takes seconds of your time to send these lost souls into the light. In those few seconds hundreds of lost souls find their way into the light. By helping them, you are helping your own soul and the evolution of planet Earth. Sounds like a big job, doesn't it? If you view it as helping others, in reality it's not a job at all. It's simply loving others.

If you feel uneasy or not sure about doing this, you can talk to a metaphysical person, someone who has done it before or you can write to me. I will be more than happy to answer any of your questions or to assist you in any way I can. When you help your-self and others in a positive way, you are exerting a positive influence on the planet.

Love your residence with all thy heart and soul and you can be a great benefit to those around you, both on the Earth plane and in the spirit world. It is your choice how much you can accomplish while you are here.

Think of yourself in their shoes as these souls wander the Earth plane searching for a way out. They can't speak with you on the material plane because most people can't hear them. They can't speak with loved ones who are in the light because they cannot find the light. What these poor souls do not understand is that when they think of the light of God, the tunnel is immediately illuminated before them. Remember that thought creates. It does not matter which plane of existence you create in.

Why don't those lost souls know this? Because some souls have died tragically. They don't know they're dead and they still think they have to eat and drink to survive. Remember that when we die, we take our personalities as well as our level of evolution with us. Some of these lost souls did not learn about spirituality while they were on the Earth plane. They got too involved in the material world and did not learn about spiritual growth.

You are your own creator on Earth as well as in the spirit world. You create with your thoughts and therefore manifest your own reality. When you are on the Earth plane, you build a house by hand, but when you are within the spirit realm, you build a house by thought. If you do not like how it turned out in the spirit world, you uncreate it simply by thinking the words. Some lost souls who are wandering the Earth plane do not know that thought creates and they still try to build the house by hand. This is why it's so important for everyone to grow spiritually while in the material world because it prepares and teaches people how to create within all the dimensions of reality.

Those lost souls are allowing their fears to interfere

with their finding the light. What they have forgotten is that as soon as they think of the word *light* or God, light or God appears before them. Do not forget how powerful you are. Creation starts with a single thought. In the spirit world you can create your own heaven or hell. The Earth plane is no different. Learn to be open-minded and you will know without a doubt why you are at your present place of residence.

Love Your Experiences

Love Your Experiences

*E*mbrace your experiences with all thy heart and soul. The person you are now is a direct result of all your experiences both in this lifetime and in past lives. As you learn from your experiences while on the Earth plane, you evolve. You are within this material environment on planet Earth because you still have lessons to master. In each lifetime you evolve more and more until you have mastered life within the physical dimension which we call Earth. The ultimate goal of your soul is to merge back with the Creator or source, who is God. Your soul is eager to return home, but it knows it first needs to experience and master its lessons. Returning home is the same as returning to God.

The path home to God is first reached by mastering this physical dimension and then by evolving through the higher dimensions or realms of consciousness. You go through many levels of reality because God has many mansions in his kingdom. The Earth plane or material dimension is considered the lower level, and therefore, all humans have a long way to go. As you're initiated and advance through the higher levels, you move closer to the home of God. When you've gone on vacation and are driving home, did you ever feel the excitement stirring within because you were eager to return home? This is the same feeling your soul or spirit feels as it learns its lessons and evolves closer and closer to its spiritual home.

When you begin to transcend beyond the third level of dense physical reality and into the higher dimensions, you will no longer require a solid physical embodiment. You are beginning to build your etheric lightbody and are capable of traveling in and out of different dimensions of reality. The more you radiate love, the higher your etheric body vibrates and the more light you can hold.

To master life within this physical reality, you must be able to balance all your bodies; that is: your physical, mental, emotional and spiritual bodies. No matter what you experience within this Earth plane, you're always able to maintain balance at all times. That is the secret for living life on planet Earth. You might require no further incarnations in a physical body, but you might want to assist others in the material world. In such a state, you would be able to either materialize or dematerialize your physical body at will.

Your higher self chooses the people whom you meet in your lifetime. Your higher self knows it needs to learn something from these individuals. Sometimes a person comes into your life to learn something from you. One way to master life on this planet is to embrace what I've described as the first commitment of love. If you do this, all the other commitments fall into place.

When experiences with others are not pleasant, it means that one or both of you need to learn something. Sometimes a person learns a lesson after a relationship is finished. After people have parted, they have time to ponder their experiences.

Here is an example. A friend of mine whom I will call Bill was involved in a relationship with Lisa. They were not married but they did live together. Bill adored Lisa and placed her high on a pedestal. Bill handed Lisa his paycheck each week in order to pay the bills and Lisa handed him back an allowance. Bill stopped visiting his friends because Lisa wanted them to spend all their time together. That was fine with Bill because he loved Lisa so much. Bill even stopped pursuing some of his favorite hobbies so they could do more together.

The relationship continued in this way for five years until Lisa dropped the bomb. She was seeing someone else behind Bill's back. Lisa informed Bill that she had never really loved him, was just using him and wanted out of the relationship. Because they were living in Lisa's apartment and her name was on the lease, Bill had to leave. He had no money because he had handed over his paychecks to Lisa for five years. When he confronted Lisa, she surprisingly said, "I don't know what you're talking about." Bill left confused, hurt, angry, sad, bitter and with just the clothes in his suitcase.

Luckily his brother, Harry, let him stay at his place until Bill got on his feet. Bill had trouble eating, sleeping and functioning at his job. Harry told him that Lisa wasn't worth it and that he should get on with his life. Bill didn't want to accept those words because he still loved Lisa and wanted her back. He missed her dearly and was willing to apologize for anything he might have done wrong. Bill didn't have any new friends and his old friends didn't call because he had dropped them five years before. Bill was very lonely and couldn't stop thinking of Lisa. He constantly felt that he had to call her.

About a month later, Bill decided to phone Lisa and try to get back together with her. Bill was so nervous that he dialed her phone number five times without it ringing for practice before he actually called. Finally Bill got up enough nerve to let the phone ring. To his terrible surprise, a man answered the phone. Bill immediately hung up and had to face the truth. Lisa was not thinking about him nor did she want him back. Harry tried to comfort Bill by taking him out to meet other girls but Bill was not interested in anyone. Bill appeared to be a lost soul in a world of his own. He was filled with despair and self-pity, and had low self-esteem and a lack of self-love.

Many people have been or are still in Bill's position. Sometimes it takes years for people to pick themselves up and move forward with their lives. Bill eventually moved on but had experienced a very painful lesson. He became bitter and distrusting of other people. Bill's bitterness and resentment spread to all those with whom he came in contact.

Eventually Bill met another woman but had trouble trusting her because of his past experience. Each of his relationships ended in the same way and the cycle continued. When the relationship ended with Lisa, Bill should have reassessed himself. By doing so he could have saved himself many more unnecessary years of heartache.

Bill's lesson for his soul's evolvement was simply to learn to love himself. Not having self-love began his downfall. Bill lost his money, the roof over his head, his friends and most of all himself. Bill depended on Lisa for his happiness, and by doing this he created a dependency, an attachment and a fear of losing Lisa. If Bill had loved himself first, he would have sensed in the beginning that Lisa was not good for him and was only out for herself.

When you love yourself unconditionally, you attract like people. When you do not love yourself, you attract people who don't love themselves. In Bill's case, his higher self was attracted to Lisa so he could learn this simple lesson of self-love. If you love yourself unconditionally, you will feel irritated or uncomfortable around someone who doesn't.

Since Bill did not learn this lesson during or after the relationship ended with Lisa, he continued to attract the same type of women. Bill was not sure what he was doing wrong. I hope that he learns this simple lesson in this lifetime or he will have to carry it with him to the next lifetime. Lisa also has to learn this lesson. If she already had, she would have never treated Bill so poorly. You love and treat others in the same manner that you love and treat yourself.

Love your experiences because without them you wouldn't be able to move forward or evolve. Remember that if things are not going well in your relationship with a friend or loved one, you must take time out to analyze what is going on and why. You will most likely find your answer. The problem with some people is they think it's always the other person's fault while they themselves are perfect. This is their lower self or ego speaking. There is no such thing as fault or right or wrong answers. Situations and obstacles come into your life for the purpose of teaching you.

When people continually place blame on others, they probably need to reevaluate themselves. If you love yourself, you will realize that there is no such word as *fault* or *blame*. These words belong to the lower self, the third dimension of human beings and the home of the ego self. A person's ego always wants to be at the top no matter what. What people do not realize is that in their materialistic illusion, the top is merely a mirror image of the bottom. Both planes flip in an instant and you never really know which is which.

When a person's ego or lower self is in charge, it always tries to be the whole ball game and forgets that other players are in the game as well. It forgets that a whole team is involved. When you learn to gently place the ego self behind you, your higher self guides the way to a higher path or truth. When you learn to tame the ego, you evolve to a higher level of being.

The ego self is concerned about being number one and forgets that we are all of one mindedness. The ego always insists that it's right and forgets that there are no right or wrong ways of being. The ego is connected to the material world whereas the higher self has dominion over the higher dimensions of reality. The ego self is concerned about material wealth whereas the higher self is concerned about spiritual growth and the soul's evolution. The ego self lives in fear that others will know more than it does or have more than it has, whereas the higher self resides within the vibrations of love and knows that knowledge and abundance are to be shared with others. The ego self tries to trick the mind into thinking that others are separated by creed, race or sexual preference whereas the higher self knows that we are all created equal in God's eyes. The ego self tries to control and manipulate others for the satisfaction of being king or master. The higher self knows that a true king or master holds no scepter and does not place others below him or herself.

A master teaches others to think for themselves and does not demand that others follow him. A master does not claim his truth is the only one to follow. A master allows students to gather knowledge and then follow their own truth in their own time. A master focuses on helping others so that others can become masters. A true master shares knowledge with students and allows them to absorb that knowledge and apply it in their own way. A student can also share his knowledge with his master and in this way becomes the master's teacher.

When we think we know everything, we need to think again. Learning does not stop within the Earth plane because God himself continues to learn and experience new ways to create. Since we're all a division of God, he sends his divided selves (our souls) out to create and experience. We then evolve and so does God.

An ascended master is here to help and assist the human race. An ascended master is fully Christ realized and therefore has mastered life at the physical level and beyond. Ascended masters no longer require food for their energy source. Their physical bodies and clothes are turned into light and they drop the physical vehicles in order to acquire lightbodies.

A lightbody is a body created from light which a person has manifested throughout all his incarnations.

An ascended master has the ability to materialize or dematerialize on any level of consciousness.
Ascension is the merging of oneness with all living beings, creatures and God.

We ascend when we have achieved a certain level of being. Such ascension depends on how quickly we have learned and applied our lessons on the physical reality. Our experiences bring us closer and closer to achieving ascension. Because vibrations are changing so rapidly on this planet at this time, more people are capable of achieving ascension in this lifetime.

Do not waste more time wondering what you did right or wrong. Embrace your experiences and mentally thank the people who either came into your life or left it. If it weren't for them, you would not be able to experience your lessons or assess what you still need to work on or identify what you have already mastered.

The experiences you had with these people taught you who you are or who you are not. As you become more enlightened, you will find that your life is a glorious and most joyous adventure. It is your choice as to what you do with your adventures once you have experienced them. Don't concern yourselves with your negative ego. Focus your energies on your spiritual growth and the evolvement of your soul. Now that you have this knowledge, go out and experience.

Languages and words are used in the material world. The spirit realm communicates with harmonics

through musical notes, light and vibration. Words
that are considered negative within the Earth plane
vibrate at lower frequencies and contain lower harmonics. They have very little light. Words of love are
created only in higher frequencies and are filled with
light. Love's harmonic sounds can radiate within all
dimensions. We must learn to leave our egos outside
the door because there is no room for it in our house
of spiritual growth.

X

Love Your
Moment of Being

Love Your
Moment of Being

L ove your moment of being with your entire
soul. Your being here is a gift from God. It is a
commitment by your soul to fulfill its own purpose.
View each moment as a learning experience so that
you can fulfill that purpose. Live in the moment and
not in the past or in the future. In the spirit world,
neither time nor space exists. Everything is created in
the moment because past and future are all one. The
reason that some psychics have a difficult time pre-
dicting a person's future is that the future can be
changed at any given moment.

Living in the past prevents you from experiencing
the moment. If you dream or ponder difficult past
events, your higher self is trying to teach you

something. Perhaps you need to clear yourself of a haunting past encounter by either physically approaching that person or by mentally visualizing them.

Some people have traumatic past experiences and because of them, have trouble in their present lives. These past experiences have been stored deep within their subconscious minds and are released into the present moment when a clearing needs to take place. Traumatic past experiences are stored in the emotional, spiritual and physical bodies as well as in the cellular memory.

A clearing is a freeing or releasing of one's self from stored up emotions caused by a difficult past experience. Sometimes when we run into a person who has deeply hurt us in the past, we immediately recall the sad events. We might have parted from this person with hard and resentful feelings. Those negative feelings penetrate deep within the subconscious mind. At certain times, the deep, hurt feelings are relived and brought into a present moment of being.

I call these haunting experiences because every now and then, our minds trigger and regenerate the memories and bring them into our conscious awareness. Our emotions trigger them and it often feels as if time didn't move and we are experiencing the hurt feelings all over again. The memories are not haunting us but rather haunting our higher selves. Our higher selves seek desperately to clear traumatic past experiences from all the body vehicles so that they can move forward and evolve.

Sometimes a traumatic event from a past life is carried into this life in order to be resolved. For example, if you have a phobia of being closed in or you cannot catch your breath and cannot explain why, perhaps you were buried alive in a past life.

If you cannot explain why you are troubled, maybe you need to seek the advice of a qualified person who facilitates past life regressions. Such people can regress you back in time to help clear up the difficulty. This is not necessary for everyone but it may be for those who are troubled so often that it interferes with their present lives. Often a fear of falling, for example, can relate to an experience during infancy when someone dropped you or you fell yourself. I know people who can clear you of these experiences. You can contact me if you need more information.

Every event you ever experienced from birth and in past lives is stored deep within your subconscious mind. The mind is a very powerful organ that contains more data than the greatest of computers. In most circumstances, your spirit guides will blank out this information because it might distract you from fulfilling your purpose in this lifetime.

For most people, it's not necessary to access that information. Sometimes your guides are with you throughout all your lifetimes. They know what you set out to accomplish for your soul's evolvement this time around. Usually your guides feel it is of no use for you to remember who you were unless it is absolutely necessary and a clearing can help with your present life.

Past data can even be blocked from the best doctors or hypnotherapists in the world if our guides feel that a certain person is not ready for the information or that the data can harm a person in any way. Some people who are working within the higher dimensions are very capable of clearing their own past experiences if the problem concerns a memory recall from this lifetime. I have done this myself. Others with whom I associate have also done this.

I would like to give you an example of a past experience that I witnessed while attending a spiritual expo. At one of the booths, a man was lying down and was being worked on by a few practitioners of the healing arts. Suddenly, the practitioners placed the man on to the floor. When they did, he started rolling down the aisle of the expo. When he stopped, he got up off the floor and was helped back to the booth. The practitioners did a few more things to him and he thanked them, smiled and went on his way. The whole process baffled me and my curiosity was aroused. I immediately walked over to see what the whole thing was about. The practitioners were more than happy to explain the circumstances.

One of the practitioners told me that as an infant, the man had had his umbilical cord wrapped around his neck while he was in his mother's womb. At the time of the Expo, the man's body vehicle was ready to release the traumatic past experience. To do this, he was guided by the practitioners to roll down the aisle so that the cord would unwind and thereby releasing or clearing the experience from all his body vehicles as well as his cellular memory.

The man was totally unaware of the situation and was not consciously aware of what he was doing. Interestingly, the man could not explain during his present lifetime why he did not want anything around his neck, even a winter scarf. Much wonderful work like this is being accomplished today. In this particular case, the man was practically reborn, minus the umbilical cord problem.

Perhaps you have had a recent traumatic past experience, such as a breakup of a relationship. Bad memories of the relationship are still haunting you as is the memory of the other person. I suggest that if it is not possible to visit that person physically, you visit him or her within the etheric dimensions. Here's how to go about it.

First, sit silently with no distractions. Tell others not to disturb you until you are finished. (This might be difficult with children or the dog barking but try to do the best you can.) The process should take about fifteen minutes of your time. As you sit in a comfortable position either on the floor or in a chair, take a few deep breaths. After each breath, let go of the problems of the day. Repeat this until you feel very relaxed. Make sure your muscles are also relaxed.

At this point, your brain waves will be in the alpha stage, which is the portal to the spirit world.

The alpha stage means total relaxation and is achieved via physical relaxation, which leads to a calm mind. The physical world functions in the beta stage where sight, sound, smell, touch and taste is experienced. In more advanced meditations, theta brain waves can be achieved and are utilized for creativity. Also, the theta stage is used for dentistry and childbirth. A delta stage is achieved when you are unconscious or in the dream state.

Visualize a bubble of white light around your entire body. As fast as you can think it, it is already there. Some of you won't be able to see it because the bubble of light is within the etheric dimension.

Second, visualize a bright, white flame with a tint of deep blue within the center. Try to keep your mind focused on this flame. If your mind wanders outwards, gently draw it back inwards. The purpose of this exercise is to make your mind one-pointed by means of concentration and will power. Continue to focus on this brilliant flame until you are one with it.

Next, mentally or aloud, call upon your guides even though you may not know their names. They are here to help and guide you, but they need you to ask them to help because they cannot interfere with your free will. Do not be frightened. They love you dearly and are patiently awaiting your call. Ask your guides for help with this clearing process. Shortly after calling on them, you might feel or sense their presence. Now you are ready to begin your clearing process.

Call upon the other person's higher self and say his or her name silently or aloud three times. Visualize the person standing in front of you next to the burning flame. It makes no difference whether you hurt the other person or the other person hurt you. You are here at this moment to clear a past experience.

When you are ready, mentally speak your words to the other's higher self even if you might think that person doesn't want to make amends. A person's higher self is always eager to do so and that's what counts. When you feel you are ready, mentally say these words to the other's higher self:

I forgive myself for any wrongdoings or negative thoughts that I sent you either consciously or unconsciously. I forgive you (name of person) for any wrongdoings or negative thoughts that you sent me either consciously or unconsciously. Thank you for coming into my life because you have shown me who I am and who I am not. I am now releasing myself from you, as well as you from me, so we can move forward and evolve. We are now free to choose other paths. I send you light and love on your chosen path of life.

After saying these words, immediately picture yourself and the person merging within the center of the deep blue flame. The deep blue color stands for healing. You are healing a past experience. The white flame around the center stands for unconditional love of self and others. You and the other person are illuminated in total unconditional love.

For this experience to work, you have to be sincere in saying the previous words. You must believe and have faith that what you say is manifested. Do not allow your lower, doubting self to interfere and project negative thoughts. If this happens, gently push the doubting thoughts aside and they will eventually cease.

If you feel you cannot say these words, don't worry. You are not ready at this time. You will know when you are ready. Do not try to convince yourself because the words must come naturally and must be said from the heart. Also, thank your guides for their assistance because they are helping you within the etheric dimension.

After completing this healing process, you might feel a release or an uplifting feeling. Also, you might feel emotional. Don't hold any feelings back. Allow the tears to flow. Your physical body is clearing the experience along with your emotional and mental bodies. Your spiritual body is cleared because it has learned and evolved from the experience of learning the simple art of forgiveness.

If you didn't feel anything, remember that the clearing took place on a subconscious level. Everyone is different and reacts in different ways. You might even find yourself laughing hysterically. This is also a type of emotional release. Do not become worried. You're doing fine.

In any case, you are now free to move forward with your life. If you know the person is deceased or you're not sure, don't be concerned. You can still resolve a past experience. You are meeting the person within the etheric dimension and it does not matter whether he or she is living or not. When you visual-ize the other person in your mind's eye in a meditative state, you are contacting the other's higher self.

Sometimes that person's higher self is visiting you in your dreams where the higher self seeks for-giveness even though the person's lower self could never ask for it. By experiencing this lesson, you both free your souls from any karmic debts. It is impor-tant that you accomplish this in this lifetime or you will have to carry that karmic debt into the next one.

Some people think they are freed of unfinished business or hurtful feelings upon their death. This is not the truth. The universal laws of cause and effect are alive and well. That's why it's so important to forgive others no matter what they do to you. If you do not learn to do this now, your soul stays linked to their souls until the energies between you are in bal-ance. This process can take many lifetimes. Don't you think it's wise to learn the act of forgiveness at this moment of your being rather than have to carry extra baggage and karmic debts?

Some people think they have cried enough over past experiences but emotions can be more deeply rooted within the emotional body than they think. These emotions need to be released so that they don't manifest themselves in the physical body as a disease. Did you ever hear the old saying: "You've given me an ulcer"? What has occurred is that the person actually has given himself or herself an ulcer by allowing emotions to run wild.

Calming and keeping the emotional body under control are among the hardest tasks to accomplish within this physical environment. However, when we can successfully do this, we will have mastered over seventy-five percent of our problems. This is because some of us have allowed our emotional bodies to take control when our higher selves should be steering the ship. Would we let a drunken person who is both emotionally upset and clearly angry, steer the ship? If the answer is no, then why do we allow our emotional selves to take control?

People who annoy us give us a chance to learn to tame our emotional bodies. If they did not cross our paths, we would not be able to tell how we're doing. When I say cross our paths, I do not mean they have to stay on our paths. I am not saying that we shouldn't be upset when an experience arises but that we should learn to keep our emotions under control.

When people annoy you, understand that sometimes they are not intentionally doing this. They may be consciously aware or not. Remember that your higher self occasionally seeks these experiences to test you, to see how well you're doing or if you still need to work on this lesson. These so-called tests come when you least expect them, even when you think you have your emotional body under control.

Remember that you are here in this illusion strictly to experience your lessons.

True masters have control over their emotions at all times. They are neither too enthusiastic when people they heal get out of a wheelchair nor are they too emotionally distressed when their mothers die. They are neither robots nor cold people but they manage to keep their emotional bodies at even, balanced levels at all times.

This is the way to become a master of physical life. When you allow your emotions to go either way, you are out of balance and out of control. Everyone has the potential to become a master but it is up to you if you want to accept this path or not.

How quickly you want to master this physical environment is totally your decision. The lower or ego self will tell you it's too much work while the higher self graciously accepts the challenge. When you feel your emotions going up and down, perhaps your lower and higher selves are dueling it out and striving to be in control. The winner will be whichever you want to win.

Love your moment of being for it is giving you a chance to experience all that is. When you sit and close your eyes, you are one with creation. When you experience this with your entire being, you will know that you are one with all beings on planet Earth.

Every person is a separate bubble experiencing for himself or herself but all people come from the same bubble container. When combined, all individuals equal a whole. Awaken and remember who you are, for you are a divine part of all that is. Every cell in your body vibrates to sounds and responds to vibrations from the universe. Who you are now can be changed at any time and space in a holy instant. Do not wait for death to wake you up.

Learn to be in the moment and not in the future. It's okay to dream of things you want or places that you would like to visit but remember to live in the now. When you visualize and fantasize about a physical object that would bring you great happiness, make sure that having it will hurt no one. In this way, you are utilizing the creative forces of the universe.

You are manifesting and drawing this future object into fruition in the now. Ask and you shall receive. You cannot sit on your front porch waiting for a thing to arrive. You have to take action and pursue what you want and thank God in advance for giving it to you. Sometimes it will take days, weeks, months or years for something to arrive, but you will know when your plane has landed.

Some people think that they have to suffer and give all their abundance away for God to accept them. Where did God say this and if you think he did, why would he give freely of his abundance and then take it away? Then he would be a punishing and judgmental God. From whom would he take the abundance and to whom would he give it?

Some people think that because something is

written in the Bible, it must be true. Did God himself write those words or truths? Hasn't the truth been rewritten? Haven't words been added and taken out during different time periods? Is this not simply another human being's truth, whether that person is a saint, master or student, or not? A true saint or master would say, "Here is my written truth or Bible; take of it as you wish. Then go find your own truth."

This book is written by me and channeled from my spirit guides. It is my truth to the best of my knowledge, but you may do with it as you wish. Is this considered to be a holy book? What is the difference between this book, another book or the Bible?

There is no difference, because all of these books were written by a human being and channeled from the spirit world. The only possible difference could be that some people force the Bible on others and preach that it is the only truth; whereas this book (as well as some others) is given to people to decipher for themselves.

The word *holy* means consecrated, saintly, blessed, sacred and godly. We have created the word *holy* and given meaning to it. It is our choice as to whether a cover of a book should have the word holy on it. Because the word *holy* is on the cover, we can't assume it is law or the only truth. The book is just considered to be holy by the person who has written it.

God has given you free will to be, gather knowledge and then live your own truth. This book is about commitments and not commandments. Commitment means involvement. You have a choice to involve yourself with this knowledge or not. You are not commanded to do so.

When we live in the past or in the future, we are missing the glorious moments of today. The future is forever changing and the past is what brought us here today. The past is gone and has already changed. Our future changes as we change but the moment is always the moment. Let's experience the moment and love our moments of being.

Our past contains some precious memories of when we were kids and had no worries. When we were kids, we often had too much fun to worry. At our present moment of being, we realize that we can choose to worry or not.

The past is filled with fun times. The future is an unknown; we might not be there. The time for fun and laughter is in this very moment.

conclusion

I hope you enjoyed *The Ten Commitments of Love* and learned many things, including who you are and why you are here. Take what you need of this knowledge and apply it in your life. If it resonates with your soul, you will know you have chosen a higher path. My purpose is to reach as many people as possible. I wish to awaken them and remind them who they are.

I cannot stress enough how much Mother Earth needs our help. Everyone senses and feels something is happening but no one is sure what to do. Sometimes a person thinks that he is too small or just one person and therefore can't make a difference. If you have read this far, you know better. You know you have an important purpose to fulfill while you are here. That purpose is to raise your consciousness so that all people can evolve to a new race of beings.

Loving others with no conditions helps raise the

vibrations tremendously upon this planet and has a direct, positive impact on Mother Earth. This does not mean there will not be changes happening to planet Earth. It does mean that we as human beings have the power to lessen the severity of these changes. Love is the answer to all things. Love is what it's all about because without it, where would we be?

If you are reading this book, you are not ready to go home yet. I don't say this with the intention of sounding mean in any way. What I'm saying is that if you were totally self-realized, you would already be home. You are here at this time to learn to be an avatar, which is a self or God-realized being from birth.

Each incarnation brings us closer to that reality. To be total self or God-realized means to live in unconditional love, absolute selflessness, compassion and service to all people. As avatars we would have the ability to extend our lives, be in many places simultaneously, produce material objects at will, have control over the five functions and five senses of our bodies and over the five elements of nature.

At this time of being, all people have to be responsible for their thoughts, words and actions. This takes practice, dedication, patience and desire, but it can be done. How do you think others have become ascended masters or avatars? It is from spiritual practice, discipline, dedication, patience and unconditional love for self, others and all creation.

If you think it's impossible to change the world, the world will not change. By thinking this, you limit your thinking. There are no limits to what you can do when you utilize the powers God has given you in a positive and loving way. Never underestimate the human mind, heart or spirit, because each of these has no limitations.

Upon arriving into this physical dimension, we relinquished our memories of ourselves. By doing so we have forgotten who we are and why we're here, and we tend to think that we are separate from others.

It is difficult for some of us to hear this knowledge now because we have already lived through many years of our lives. However, if we knew who we were at birth, would we have learned who we are now? There would have been no lessons for us to experience here. Such knowledge would defeat our purpose for being here. We are here because there are still lessons left for us to master. Otherwise, we would not need to be here. I am here because I know I have lessons left to master. When I master those lessons, I'm sure there will be still more to learn.

The difficult time you had, or are still experiencing, is for the single purpose of mastering a lesson. There will always be things to learn but once you have mastered life within the physical dimension, you will have a choice of what you do next. The choices can include being of service within the etheric dimension, reincarnating back to the Earth plane to help others or learning lessons on other planets, in other galaxies and universes. Your progress depends on how quickly you learn your lessons. It all starts with the first commitment in this book. Remember that you chose to be here at this time. You wanted the opportunity to experience and be part of the exciting times ahead.

The transition into the year 2000 and beyond is a time of opportunity for self-renewal. We know what either has or has not worked for us. We have a chance to create a New World order and create balance, harmony, love and peace all over the planet.

Other beings from different star systems have been gathering here to help us through this great transition. Some of the regions of assisting star systems include the Pleiades, Sirius, Omega Orion and Arcturus.

The Pleiades is a cluster of stars often referred to as the seven sister stars. Pleiadians are here to warn us about our animalistic natures and tell us that we are destroying the ecological environment on planet Earth. They are also here to help us with our spiritual growth so that we can evolve.

The star constellation of Sirius houses the office of the Christ and Melchizedek consciousness. Omega Orion is a majestic entrance to regions containing pure energy. Arcturus is the brightest star and contains one of the most advanced civilizations in our galaxy.

The Alpha Centaurians are also here. They have

scientific and technical knowledge to share with us. Their mission is to help us understand this knowledge because they are more advanced technologically than we are.

Two great beings of light called Master Enoch and Metatron are here too. They are preparing the human race for the quantum leap. This leap will effect every level of intelligence upon planet Earth.

Archangel Michael is working within the etheric dimensions and is in charge of the Great White Brotherhood. As soon as you call on Archangel Michael, you can feel his presence of unconditional love. I call upon him often to help me with my clearing work.

It is time for people of planet Earth to realize that there are beings from other planets, star systems, galaxies and other universes who are here. What makes you think that Earth is the only planet that houses life? Who told you that? Your ego is the main culprit because it wants to be the only one. The ego tricks you into thinking no other life exists. Some people deny that other forms of life exist because they fear the unknown.

Let's expand our consciousness and place our egos and fears behind us. Let's stop limiting our thinking. These beings of light admire us and are anxiously awaiting our calls for help. They are here to help and assist us but we must first help ourselves.

Seasons and weather patterns have changed dramatically and continue to be more severe. Perhaps we should all begin to take heed of Mother Earth's warnings and hear her cries. Mother Earth is also going through a major cleansing and releasing of stored up emotions from all the abuse she has ingested and continues to ingest.

What happens when we give our vehicles bad or low-grade gasoline and forget to change the oil or get a tune-up? We think our vehicles will last forever. We also think nothing will happen to us. Some of us do this because we are lazy or lack funds. Some people simply don't care. When a vehicle breaks down indefinitely, they borrow or purchase another one. No matter how we abuse our vehicles, eventually they'll break down. The same is true of Mother Earth, accept we can't borrow or buy another planet.

We mistreat her year after year, decade after decade, and continue to think she will last forever. Mother Earth has been hinting to us about her circumstances by means of the intensity and severity of the disasters that have plagued this planet.

When greedy people tear down the rain forest, they in reality are taking away a large percentage of the oxygen upon this planet. Our precious rain forest is the main source of oxygen for our whole planet. What happens when we take out the main source? God's message is clear and simple. We are to love each other. Does God need to rock this planet for us to hear or feel that we need to change our ways?

A thought is created in a holy instant. Words follow. Action is taken within minutes. That's how fast we could change this world. Perhaps there are places on Earth that have already manifested heaven. Let's have the entire planet be heaven. Let's become the advanced human beings that we were meant to be so that we can join our neighboring star systems.

Some advanced beings took part in the creation of the ancient pyramids of Egypt and offered the Egyptians advanced medical knowledge. Do you think they have any good advice or anything worth listening to now? I ask you because I want you to learn to think for yourself. These beings of light have so much to share but it is up to every individual to pick up the phone and to utilize this knowledge wisely.

Advanced beings have witnessed what we have done with our weaponry and all the destruction it has caused others on this planet. The vibrations have been felt all the way to the center of Earth and as far as other universes. These light beings are patiently waiting for us to become advanced spiritually before they share scientific and technological knowledge with us. They want to make sure we are capable of handling the information and that we don't use it for war or destruction.

The testing of warheads deep within the Earth's crust has vibrated, rippled and entered into the inter-dimensions. All beings that are in the spirit world as well as other star systems and universes want to make sure that we do not destroy ourselves and planet Earth. These advanced beings know that everything (including themselves) is created by God. Did you think God only created the human vehicle?

The father's house of many mansions is unfolding before us. We decide which mansion we want to reside in. Help spread the word about this book to others so they have an opportunity to utilize this knowledge. Let *The Ten Commitments of Love* reach around the entire planet so we can all see and hear God's simple message of love.

I, Michele Mack, send you blessings on your glorious journey through life.

.   .   .

Here's a prayer that you can say each day to help raise the vibrations and assist in the healing of Mother Earth. The more people that say this prayer, the easier it will be for everyone as a group consciousness. Wherever you may live upon this planet, say this prayer at 8:00 PM. (This includes all time zones). Doing so will create a ripple effect around planet Earth as well as within the etheric dimensions. If you only say one prayer, make it this one. Carry this prayer with you and place it in your wallets. Don't leave home without it.

I AM SENDING LIGHT AND LOVE UPON MOTHER EARTH

After you say these words, immediately visualize a

beam of light filled with love coming from your heart and radiating out into the world. The angels will take that light to where it's needed for healing. Know that it is done. Do not allow any negative thinking to interfere with this process. It will take only a few seconds of your time but the results will be monumental. God's divine plan is being anchored on Earth and it is an exciting moment for the future of our beloved planet.

About the Author

*M*ichele Mack, author of *The Ten Commitments of Love*, is a teacher, healer and writer.

Michele's key message is "A thought is created in a holy instant, words are shortly followed and action is taken within minutes. That's how fast we could change this world!"

The author is an ordained minister in the Order of Melchizedek from the Sanctuary of the Beloved.

This is a group of 8000-plus individuals who come from all walks of life as well as many different countries. Their mission is a commitment to teaching and healing the human condition and serving the people upon planet Earth in almost every way where Light is needed. This Order is not bound by creeds or doctrines. It functions by free will for healing and teaching wherever one is guided.

Michele is also a practitioner of Reiki and Seichim. Reiki refers to the life energy within us all.

Reiki helps each individual release energy blocks and the connected emotions, which in turn helps release the causal level of disease. Seichim represents love and courage at the highest universal dimensions. When given Seichim energy, every molecule and subatomic particle in the subtle and physical bodies is positively affected.

Michele currently resides in Pennsylvania and continues to make her contribution to planet Earth by healing, teaching and writing. She was guided to write this book because so many people need to hear its words. Michele is currently preparing a children's series which will be released later this year.

INDEX

A

Abuse, 31-33

Abusive relationships, 30, 32

Alpha Centaurians, 150

Anderson, George, 84

Angels, 60, 113, 115

Archangel Michael, 151

Arcturus, 150

Ascend, 129

Ascended masters, 60, 64, 75, 128-129, 148

Authority, 37, 53

B

Beings of light, 60-63, 75, 114, 151, 153

Brotherhood of light, 75

C

Channeling, 61, 75, 114, 145

Clearing, 134

Comfort zone, 76, 80-81, 98

Competition, 7-9, 28

Convenience foods, 40

D

Death, 82-83, 86, 106

Disability, 12

E

Earth plane, 122

Ego self, 126-127, 143

Etheric dimensions, 138-140, 149

Evolvement, 74, 77, 100

Evolving, 100

F

Failure, 76

Fear, 7-10, 20-22, 25-26, 29-31, 49-50, 55, 63, 71, 78, 89, 97-98

Fourth dimension, 72

G

Gay people, 25-27

God, 47-55, 71, 74-75, 121-122, 128

Great beings of light, 151

Great White Brotherhood 75, 151

H

Hierarchy, 60, 64, 113

Higher dimensions, 72-73, 121

Higher levels, 122

Hurtak, J.J. , 78

I

"I AM," invocation, 71, 154

J

Jesus, 52

L

Levels, 70

Levels of reality, 121

Light, 71

Light beings, 113, 153

Lightbody, 128

Love vibration, 15, 28, 71

Lower level, 122

M

Master Enoch, 151

Metatron, 151

Minority, 24

O

Omega Orion, 150

Organic, 42

farmers, 42

produce, 41

soil, 38

Organic food, 42

P

Paradise, 65

Past experience, 134, 136, 141

Past life regressions, 135

Pleiades, 150

Possessions, 8

Prejudice, 25-26

R

Red meat, 40, 42

Relationship of nonattachment, 27-28

Religion, 47-50, 64, 71-72

Retire, 93

Retirement, 92-94, 102

S

Secret to the universe, 51

Simplicity in life, 39

Sirius, 150

Soul, 100

Soul's evolvement, 74, 100
125

Stone, Dr. Joshua David,
64, 78, 96

T

Third dimension, 73, 126

Third level of reality, 72,
122

U

Universal law of
attraction, 24

V

Vegetarians, 40

Vibration, 62, 70, 101

Vibrational level, 24, 40

Vibrations of love, 99

Visit, 137

ORDER FORM

Postal orders: Covenant of Light Publishing
Attn: Michele Mack
119 Mertz Road
Mertztown, PA 19539 USA

Please return this portion with payment

....

YES, I want *The Ten Commitments of Love*!

Please send me _____ copies at $12.95 each,
plus $4 shipping for one book and $2 for each additional book.
(PA residents only please include 6% sales tax)

Name:_____

Company name: _____

Address:_____

City:_____ State: _____ Zip: _____

Telephone: (_____)_____
(In case we have any questions about your order.)

Check or money order payable to: Covenant of Light Publishing
119 Mertz Road, Mertztown, PA 19539

....

THANK YOU FOR YOUR ORDER!

If you have any comments or questions about this book,
please feel free to write the author. All letters will be answered.

Sorry, we're not accepting credit cards. This is a team effort to
keep everyone's debts down and so begins the ripple effect!
It's as simple as that.

Phone: (610) 641-0298 Fax: (610) 682-7866
E-mail: covltpub@aol.com

Postal orders: Covenant of Light Publishing
Attn: Michele Mack
119 Mertz Road
Mertztown, PA 19539 USA

Please return this portion with payment

. . . .

YES, I want *The Ten Commitments of Love*!
Please send me _____ copies at $12.95 each,
plus $4 shipping for one book and $2 for each additional book.
(PA residents only please include 6% sales tax)

Name:_____

Company name: _____

Address:_____

City:_____ State: _____ Zip: _____

Telephone: (_____)_____
(In case we have any questions about your order.)

Check or money order payable to: Covenant of Light Publishing
119 Mertz Road, Mertztown, PA 19539

. . . .

THANK YOU FOR YOUR ORDER!
If you have any comments or questions about this book,
please feel free to write the author. All letters will be answered.

Sorry, we're not accepting credit cards. This is a team effort to
keep everyone's debts down and so begins the ripple effect!
It's as simple as that.

Phone: (610) 641-0298 Fax: (610) 682-7866
E-mail: covltpub@aol.com